PROMOTIONS MADE EASY

PROMOTIONS
MADE EASY

A STEP-BY-STEP GUIDE
TO THE EXECUTIVE SUITE

STACY MAYER

FOREWORD BY ELEANOR BEATON

HOUNDSTOOTH
PRESS

Editors: Marie Hanifen and Stacy Booth

Author Photo: In Her Image Photography

Names in this book have been changed to ensure privacy and confidentiality.

Visit stacymayer.com/resources to download free promotion guides, learn more about Stacy's executive coaching programs, and join her training webinars.

Executive Ahead of Time is a registered trademark of Stacy Mayer Consulting LLC.

PROMOTIONS MADE EASY

A Step-by-Step Guide to the Executive Suite

ISBN   978-1-5445-2524-2 *Hardcover*

978-1-5445-2522-8 *Paperback*

978-1-5445-2523-5 *Ebook*

978-1-5445-2525-9 *Audiobook*

For my mom, who told me that I could do and be anything I wanted in life. She was right.

CONTENTS

ACKNOWLEDGMENTS 9

FOREWORD 11

INTRODUCTION 15

1. A PROMOTION IS NOT A REWARD FOR YOUR HARD WORK ..25

2. STOP DOING WHAT YOU'RE GOOD AT 35

3. STRATEGIC THINKING VS. STRATEGY 61

4. THE CASE FOR 3×ING YOUR CAREER VISION 75

5. DEFINING YOUR LEADERSHIP STYLE.. 91

6. BUILD TRUST WITH 15-MINUTE ALLY MEETINGS 109

7. THE PERFORMANCE REVIEW PROBLEM 129

8. HOW TO ADVOCATE FOR YOUR PROMOTION 147

9. HOLDING YOURSELF ACCOUNTABLE 169

10. HOW YOU'LL KNOW IF IT'S WORKING 189

11. OVERCOMING YOUR FEAR OF FAILURE................................ 209

CONCLUSION 221

ACKNOWLEDGMENTS

My heartfelt thanks and gratitude to everyone who helped me bring this book to life. My loving husband, Timothy Ham, who believed in the power of this work and kept telling me to "just write the darn book." My mom has always been my biggest fan, and when I told her I was finally writing a book, her words were, "It's about time." My father, who also said, "Of course you are." My editor, Marie Hanifen, who, let's be real, was way more than an editor. My countless coaches and mentors who have guided and supported me throughout the years: Eleanor Beaton, Stacey Boehman, Moksha, Tracy Litt, Laura Swartzbaugh, Leila Bulling Towne, and Kerrie Halmi. And to my incredible clients who not only trusted me to guide their careers but allowed me to challenge and support them to show up as their badass selves every single day. I love you all.

FOREWORD

BY ELEANOR BEATON, CEO, SAFI MEDIA

When I was thirty-four years old, I spent three days shadowing a woman widely considered to be one of Canada's top executives as she vacationed in her hometown. We were collaborating on what would become one of the most celebrated business books in the nation the year it was released. But that humid July, we had no idea how successful our collaboration would become. We were a thirty-something and a fifty-something, getting groceries, visiting people, and talking through the mistakes, triumphs, and strategies that had shaped her brilliant career.

We visited artists, museums, community centers, and a university. We stopped in corner stores and ice cream stalls. Everywhere we went, people were delighted to see her. The feeling was mutual. She asked after people's parents and children. She requested status updates on meaningful projects and initiatives. As I observed one conversation after another, I heard her offering support and encouragement, as well as shrewd business and leadership advice. And I also realized that this woman had been quietly offering not only strategic counsel to these community-based organizations, but funding—from her own pockets—as well. In addition to running billion-dollar companies, this astonishing female executive had been redistributing her wealth and know-how to hundreds of deserving people and community organizations for decades.

The final stop on our "tour" was the humble workshop of a local woodworker. This female executive had successfully nominated the artist to receive an "Order of Canada"—one of the country's highest honors. As a parting gift, she bought me one of his creations—a magnificent wooden bowl. "It can be a memento of our time together," she said as we pulled out of his yard. The bowl sits on my desk today as a reminder of the single most important lesson I learned from that female executive: when women earn, we all win.

Getting promoted to senior executive roles isn't only about getting more money and status (although both those things are great, dahling). The greatest benefit you will reap from your promotion is the woman you become in the process. A woman who demonstrates that empathy and connection are the true seat of power. A woman who understands that having power is meaningless unless you deploy it to uplift others.

What you hold in your hands is a clear and uncompromising guide to help you achieve tremendous career success while loving the woman you become in the process. I can think of no truer guide to help you in your career than Stacy Mayer. Her brilliant book will help you amass external success—pay raises, promotions, and professional accolades—but it will also show you how to build the inner resilience you need to not only sustain that success over the long term, but share your success with tens, hundreds, or thousands of others.

Read the book, apply the lessons, and tell every woman you know about it. When women earn, we all win.

INTRODUCTION

You've read a lot of books that tell you how to be a better leader. Still, you stay right where you are—raising your hand, asking for more. Yet nothing changes. You might even be in a leadership position right now, but you still struggle to pull yourself out of the weeds.

What is that one missing piece in your career development?

There is a chasm between where you are right now and the leader you want to become—a chasm that you need to cross first, but might not even know is there. You sense it because sometimes it's right in front of your face. It's when you get a glowing performance review but not a promotion. It's when your colleague's title changes but yours doesn't. It's when you receive a special project but no additional compensation.

This book gives you a step to the missing piece. I'm going to show it to you, and you'll be able to cross that chasm. In the blink of an eye, you'll be on the other side.

And it is glorious.

I was a cookie-cutter corporate coach for many years. I taught leadership skills, time management, and things like that—things that made my clients better managers. And they did become better, more effective managers. But what they also got was more work and more responsibility—and they didn't get the recognition or the larger voice at their organization. They didn't get the "seat at the table" that their better management skills were supposed to bring. I felt disappointed, like my clients did, that more leadership skills didn't result in leadership positions.

As a coach, I didn't just want corporate women to become better managers. I wanted them to get recognized for their talents and hard work. Get promotions! A seat at the table! I wanted them to feel fulfilled.

So I started to coach on more than typical "leadership skills." I realized that being the hardest worker doesn't lead to a promotion, but...

deliberately managing your career, and your life, does.

I taught women to take charge of their promotion, instead of being led by their boss. And as I helped more and more clients reach their dream positions, some of them reaching the C-suite and beyond, patterns started to emerge.

Through this work I uncovered a step-by-step process that takes corporate women to the executive level. These are women who have gone from underappreciated, under-recognized, and underpaid to becoming a valued member of the leadership team. And throughout this book, I will show you how to do that as well.

Promotions are easy using my process outlined in this book, and if you aren't where you want to be, you simply have been focused on the wrong things.

Before we dive into all of the amazing tools and strategies I have outlined in this book, I want to share with you a few misconceptions my clients held when we first met that were holding them back from reaching that next level of success.

#1: MY COMPANY ALREADY HAS A PROFESSIONAL DEVELOPMENT PLAN IN PLACE FOR ME.

This is a super common misconception. Many people tell me that their company already has a professional development plan and they're working through it with human resources as we speak. But things aren't quite moving as fast as they would like them to.

Many organizations have a mission to develop talent. They truly want to support their employees and give them opportunities. Perhaps you have been tagged as a high potential leader, which is great. Maybe they have even sent you to a few leadership courses. This is also great. But at the end of the day, you still aren't getting promoted. And that is because of one thing:

Organizations care about their own bottom line.

Your organization cares more about you hitting your targets in your current position than giving you a promotion. They care about you doing a great job in your role. And getting you into a higher-level executive position is simply not their top priority. You are the only person who cares about you.

Start to think about that. I really want you to understand, especially if you're relying on your company's professional development plan to get ahead. If you're relying on your performance reviews to get you to that next level, you're still going to be sitting exactly where you are wondering what the heck happened.

This book is all about putting you into the driver's seat and teaching you how to use the opportunities in front of you.

Use all of your company resources, programs, and awards, but ultimately take matters into your own hands.

#2: I AM WORKING WITH MY BOSS TO GET PROMOTED.

Remember, *you're the only person who cares about you getting promoted*—not your boss, and not anyone else at your organization. And that's a good thing. It's okay. So just know that it's your job. It's your job to put yourself out there. If you want to be in a higher-level leadership position, if you feel like you want to get the recognition that you deserve, if you want to get paid for your ideas instead of the hours that you put in at work, if you want to build out a stronger team, if you want to create boundaries, if you want to have success once you make it into that position, it is up to you.

My client Sharon is a finance manager at a medium-size company in Canada. Her boss, the CEO, genuinely wants her to become the CFO someday. But it's up to her to own what that position is going to look like. And she is so lucky that she has a boss who is willing to create that for her. But if she doesn't ask for it, if she doesn't lay out the plan, if she doesn't create the org chart, he isn't going to create it for her.

So that is your job. You need to care about your professional development and set yourself up for success.

#3: I HAVE BEEN ACTIVELY SEEKING A PROMOTION FOR A WHILE NOW.

Have you been working to get better at your job by putting in more hours and more of your energy? Then you haven't actually been going for a promotion. This one might not be fun to hear. You might be saying, "Yes, I am. I have done everything I can do."

Yet your actions don't match it. As you're reading this book, I really want you to start asking yourself, *Am I really going for a promotion, or am I just spending time and focusing on my job and making sure that I'm good at my job and putting in the hours for my job?*

Both are valid career choices, but only one gets you promoted into the executive suite.

My mission is to bring more diversity to the leadership table by getting 1,000 powerhouse corporate women promoted into senior executive leadership positions each and every year worldwide.

I created the Executive Ahead of Time group coaching intensive in 2020 as a way to move closer to that mission.

Executive Ahead of Time is a step-by-step promotion strategy and executive coaching program that helps established corporate leaders move toward their next promotion with ease and have success once they get there. The success of this program and its graduates inspired me to write this book so that even more leaders can put my process into action.

Now with every woman that I coach to become a corporate badass, they not only land that executive level promotion, but they have the skills to thrive in the executive suite.

Let me further define what I mean by corporate badass.

A corporate badass is my client Diana, who is also a global citizen. Diana was born in Eastern Europe and immigrated to the United States while in college. She hired me when she was the director of finance at a global retail organization. Diana came to me very happy with what she had achieved so far in her career, but she also knew that she was ready for more.

As part of my coaching process, I assess where each of my clients sees themself long term. In her case, she knew she wanted to become the CFO someday. But this goal felt out of reach, like she didn't need to think about it right now. She had decided that her immediate goal of building better relationships with her peers was more important. I showed her how we could do both.

When she made the commitment to set herself up to become the CFO while building better relationships with her peers, she officially transitioned into corporate badass status. Now

Diana proudly holds the title of chief financial officer at her organization and is making a bigger impact than she could have ever imagined just one year earlier at our first coaching conversation.

A corporate badass is Kim Blue. Kim, a thought leader, strategist, and human resources professional, received a skip-level promotion from senior manager to vice president of people experience at one of the largest technology companies in Silicon Valley in the middle of the pandemic.

She didn't spend a moment thinking about the limitations of her current title. She knew where she aspired to be, the impact she wanted to make, and she interviewed accordingly. She understood her value as a senior executive leader, and she was able to advocate for herself to show others that value. She showed up to the interview as a corporate badass, and it paid off.

Then there is corporate badass Jennifer Fisher. Jennifer, a highly educated Virginian blonde who never leaves the house without her lipstick and a smile, has taken what it means to be a corporate badass to an entirely new level.

Jennifer reached out to me because she was very ambitious and wanted to take her career to the next level. She was currently the vice president of sales for a large study-abroad company. She received above average performance reviews, had great sales numbers, and loved her work. But we discovered early on that part of the reason she was so effective at her job was because she was very hands on. If there was a problem to be solved, she fixed it herself.

Once she committed to stepping into her leadership role by focusing on the strategic vision for her group and inspiring others to step up to the plate, she became a total corporate badass. Now she has the senior vice president role overseeing an even larger corporate initiative, and she's the host of her own podcast on sales leadership.

I have met and trained so many corporate badasses over the years. And I have developed a list of core guiding principles for my Executive Ahead of Time students to obtain corporate badass status. Here they are:

- As a corporate badass, we get promoted in half the time with less effort.
- We enjoy the process it takes to get there, and we have success once we reach that executive position.
- We learn to differentiate ourselves from others at our organization, not because of our technical skillset or tenure at our organization, but because of our significant and powerful leadership style.
- We work smarter, not harder. We know our career path and how we are going to get there, and we create allies along the way.

- We do not sell ourselves short, worry that we won't be able to do the job, or focus on what we don't know. We make bold decisions, we speak up, and we offer solutions, not just problems.
- We understand that a promotion is not a reward for our hard work. We focus on what we can control, and we take steps to get ourselves to that next level of leadership.
- Executive Ahead of Time brings more diversity to the leadership table, creating a new wave of innovation, power, and inclusivity in the corporate world.
- We don't settle for a seat at the table. We demand to have a voice. We are the next wave of leadership.
- We reshape the future of our company, and we truly are making a difference across the world.

This is not only possible for you too, but after you finish reading this book, you'll have everything you need to make that happen for yourself and become a total corporate badass in the process.

See you in Chapter 1.

A PROMOTION IS NOT A REWARD FOR YOUR HARD WORK

When I am asked, "Stacy, what's the first thing I need to do if I want to be promoted into a senior executive leadership position?" the answer is simple:

Understand that a promotion is not a reward for your hard work.

You may know this in theory. You may have even been passed over for a promotion because you relied on your hard work to speak for itself. But you still aren't living by it. Understanding this is the key to unlocking everything I will be teaching you on the subsequent pages of this book.

A PROMOTION DOESN'T *HAPPEN* TO YOU

A promotion is something you actively go out and get. It's not handed to you. You have to make it happen.

Yet part of you still believes that if you work hard, you will be rewarded.

Or perhaps you believe that if you want to make it to that next level of leadership, you just need a better boss.

Or that you just need to switch companies.

But what if it wasn't any of those things? What if you simply needed to act as if a promotion wasn't a guaranteed result of your hard work?

You are good at what you do! That's what got you here. I have no doubt that you know how to do your job. But you can't just keep doing your *job* and expect recognition to follow.

LET'S GO BACK IN TIME

Remember when you graduated college? You met with career counselors, consulted with professionals, attended job fairs, took personality tests—all the things to guarantee your success after graduation. Then somehow you got lost along the way.

You started working or maybe you started a family, and somehow you lost sight of your career. Things started happening *to* you. You stopped being proactive and became reactive instead.

Promotions came easy early on. You took opportunities as they came. But along the way, you lost sight of the number one most important thing:

YOURSELF.

What you want. What matters to you. How YOU can make the biggest impact at your organization.

You tried to make yourself feel better by turning to excuses. Excuses like:

- Title doesn't matter.
- Money doesn't matter.
- I have so much freedom.
- I am able to leave every day at 5:00 p.m.
- I have a short commute.
- I have been with my company for fifteen years.
- I just need to wait until my stock vests.
- I'll be eligible for a bonus soon.

Although each of these excuses isn't bad or wrong, they can't be the only reason you are making the decisions you are making about your career.

At this point, you are probably saying, *But Stacy! I DO take my career goals seriously. I want a promotion, but what more can I do?*

You can be doing SO MUCH MORE. Trust me.

Here's an example:

Let's take a look at your friend at work.

She sits right next to you, and you have quite a bit in common.

You're both senior managers, you both have your MBA, and you've both been at the company for about ten years.

But two weeks ago, she was promoted, and what did you get?

You got her direct reports and no additional compensation.

That's right. No promotion but lots more work to do.

As a result, you feel frustrated. You try to come up with answers for why she got promoted while you're still in the same spot. Then the excuses start.

- It's got to be because of her winning personality.
- It's got to be because she has more friends at the top.

- It's got to be because she knows how to play politics better than I do.

NO!

It's because, while you had your head down trying to get work done, she was acting as if a promotion was not a guaranteed result of her hard work.

If you are good at your job but still getting left behind, I guarantee you are making choices on the "work hard and get rewarded" mentality all day, every day.

What does the "work hard and get rewarded mentality" look like in action?

It looks like:

- Not speaking up in meetings.
- Not sharing your accomplishments.
- Only having professional development conversations at review time.
- Only taking on responsibilities associated directly with your current role.
- Answering emails at two o'clock in the morning because you're worried your boss will think you're not doing your job if you don't.
- Believing that your boss doesn't want to hear about YOU

during your one-on-ones. She just wants to know what your team is doing.

This is a REAL problem. Not just because it won't lead to a promotion, but it's also a problem because you are not actually doing your job!

If you are in any type of management role (senior manager, director, a vice president, or above), it is *your job* to think strategically. It is your job to pull yourself out of the weeds and look at the big picture. It is your job to lead by example and not by doing everything for your team.

A PROMOTION DOESN'T ALWAYS MEAN A HIGHER JOB TITLE

Here's what I mean:

I meet C-suite executives all the time who are just as frustrated as you are because they have no influence, they have no autonomy, they're always in the weeds, and nobody listens to them.

I have met senior managers who have more resources, are happier at work, and are actually getting promoted on a regular basis in terms of pay increases, responsibility, taking on projects, or having more face time with leadership. They're loving their job, and they're really making an impact at their organization, but they don't necessarily have the title to match. But they're making an impact at a really high level.

This tells me that it's not always about the title. What it *is* about is the person who you become. When you become that Executive Ahead of Time, you are embodying what it means to be an executive.

Everything in this book is about teaching you how to embody executive leadership and how to think and communicate like a senior executive leader so you can never get passed over for a promotion again.

You know exactly where you're headed. You know exactly what to do. You can pivot on command. You thrive on challenging situations. You're able to make decisions. You're able to spend more time with your family and live in abundance. This is all becoming the Executive Ahead of Time.

So let's get real here for a moment and ask yourself:

Am I actually doing my job as a leader, or am I simply managing other people's problems?

You will know the answer to this question because your results will prove it. Are you actually getting the recognition that you think you deserve at work? If the answer is no, then something is not working.

Throughout this book, I will show you the key to unlocking what *will* get you the recognition you deserve.

But let's start simple.

Because once you realize that a promotion is not a reward for your hard work, then you can *do something about it.*

CHAPTER SUMMARY

- A promotion is something that you actively go out and get—and that's a good thing. It's not necessarily just handed to you. You not only have the ability to make it happen for yourself, but also it's better that way.
- The first step toward advancing into a senior executive leadership position is to understand that a promotion is not a guaranteed result for your hard work.
- As a subject matter expert, it made sense that you were rewarded for your hard work. But this strategy no longer works at the executive level. To advance to the next level, you need to also be deliberate about your career.
- Symptoms of the "work hard and get rewarded" mentality include not speaking up in meetings, not sharing your accomplishments, only taking on responsibilities related to your current role, fielding questions and requests at all hours of the day and night, believing that your boss doesn't want to hear about you during your one-on-ones, and being good in your role but struggling to get promoted.

- Once you accept that a promotion is not a reward for your hard work and you're willing to let go of the "work hard and get rewarded" mentality, then you can take steps toward getting promoted into senior executive leadership.

CHAPTER 2

STOP DOING WHAT YOU'RE GOOD AT

The purpose of this entire book is to get you set up for your next promotion and give you the tools you need to have success once you get there. One of the most important things you're going to need to do to ensure your success at the executive level is to master the skill of getting yourself out of the weeds.

This is unbelievably important.

You might realize already that it's important to get out of the weeds simply so you can at least manage your stress levels.

Some managers can't even imagine accepting a promotion because they believe that a promotion automatically requires more work. This attitude might even result in you turning down promotion opportunities.

Because your work–life balance is so important, because you don't want to be stressed out, because you don't want everything to be about work, you turn down those opportunities.

And you can turn down work in more than one way.

You turn down work using your words by actually saying no. Or you might be turning them down energetically because you just can't take on any more responsibility.

You can't put more on your plate because you're already maxed out. You realize that even though you are turning down opportunities, you still don't have the work–life balance you desire. So it feels like nothing is really working.

If you find yourself in this situation, you're not alone.

THE TRAP OF YOUR SUBJECT MATTER EXPERTISE

Most of the managers who work with me are really amazing subject matter experts. I have clients who are at the vice president or senior vice president level who are still seen as subject matter experts.

But the problem is that it doesn't scale. If you're managing other managers, you could be managing hundreds of people. You can't possibly manage all of the details of that many people. There aren't enough hours in the day. This is why it is so important to get out of the weeds now.

As you continue to grow, if the executive team doesn't see you as somebody who can't pull themself out of the weeds, then you will never get promoted into that next level of leadership. But not anymore.

Starting today, I want you to vow with me that you are going to get yourself out of the weeds. I want you to commit and to understand how imperative this is, and also to know that it's going to take some time.

This is very, very challenging. It's a really fine line to feel like your job is on the line and you want to scale yourself. You want to put yourself out there, and you want to take on more responsibility, yet you're going to start delegating more, and you're going to start blocking out time for strategic thinking. It might feel really weird and foreign right now, but I'm telling you: once you start doing it, it is going to feel amazing, and you will be on your way to being seen as a senior executive leader.

You are going to do that by changing the way you're communicating with leadership.

Now before you say, "But my boss really WANTS to know

all the details…" even if that were true, it doesn't mean you can't start changing your communication.

How are you communicating? Are you communicating about the details all the time? Are you communicating about your scorecard now?

My client Kathryn joined Executive Ahead of Time at the most inconvenient time.

She was very busy with work. She was on the edge of burn-out. She was frustrated. She was getting sick. She didn't know where to turn.

She was maxed out and felt like she couldn't possibly join a training program. But she had known me for a few years and felt confident I could help her. So she reached out and said, "Stacy, I need some help." And I said, "Trust me. You have to join us."

I could tell she was stressed on our first group call. But by the second, she seemed a bit calmer. And all she started to do was change the way she was communicating with her boss.

She had a new boss who was part of the reason she was feeling so much stress. I coached her to speak to her boss as a peer. She stopped talking about all the details all the time, and instead she improved her communication with him and really made a connection.

Then this amazing thing happened.

She became a corporate badass. An opportunity came up from another company. They told her they needed her on their team, and they requested an interview.

And because she was working with me, she asked herself, "What would Stacy say?"

Here's what Stacy would say: Stacy would say yes to the darn interview!

So Kathryn said yes.

The next time we talked, she told me, "I literally never would have done this if it weren't for your coaching."

This all happened in the first few weeks of working together.

BEING IN THE WEEDS TELLS LEADERSHIP YOU AREN'T READY TO BE PROMOTED

If you are constantly in the details, you're basically telling leadership that you're not ready for a senior executive leadership role. As a result, they can't promote you.

It may feel weird or counterintuitive, but the leadership team simply can't promote you if you are the subject matter expert.

Here's why:

One, they don't know who else is going to do your job. This actually happened to one of my clients. I was conducting a stakeholder interview with her boss, the CEO, and in the conversation, he literally said to me, "I can't promote her because I don't have anyone else who could do her job."

This is like a shot in the foot, right? It feels really bad. It doesn't feel great to be the only one who can do your job and also to know that you got yourself into that position.

And two, all of your bad habits scale with you. If they promote you into an executive position, you're already overworked. You're already so far into the details, they know that you're not going to be able to be that high-level leader that they need you to be.

I had a CTO join my Executive Ahead of Time program for this exact reason. He had scaled all of his bad habits with him to the C-suite. Now he was mentoring a successor and guess what? His successor had all the same bad habits.

Middle manager, senior executive—I don't care who you are. If you are still putting out fires at two in the morning, if you are relying on your expertise to get ahead, if you are getting stellar ratings on your performance reviews, but you still aren't getting a promotion to match—**you have got to stop doing what you are good at.**

I had a really amazing conversation with a client about this after six months of working together.

She was telling me that when she first started coaching, she responded to every little task. Her value was in her tasks. At one point, she was trying to negotiate a pay raise, and she actually made a list of all the projects she was working on to build her business case. It didn't work.

Maybe you have done that before too? Tried to negotiate something based on all the "stuff" you have accomplished? Did it work? I'd be curious to know. My hunch is even if it did work, it likely only got you a small percent compared to what you could have earned if you truly knew your value.

Back to my client. I asked her where she was now.

She said, "Oh, I don't think about my tasks at all. I mean, I do, but that's just work. The real confidence is coming from my ideas. I am being included in the conversation. I am being pulled aside and asked for my advice now. I am confident."

Yes!!! But I never like just assuming that one is better than the other. And she was "happy" before we met. So I asked her which she thought was better.

Well for one, now she is actually doing her job as vice president. When she negotiated her pay increase AGAIN, it was a no-brainer. Her CEO said yes, of course, without batting an eye.

She also mentioned that she didn't know what she didn't know before. That she actually wasn't aware that focusing on the task instead of the strategy was KEEPING her from getting ahead.

Maybe you are there too? Either it doesn't occur to you that being a master of every single task is not part of your job if you want to be seen as a leader, OR you know you need to get out of the weeds but aren't sure how.

THE TWO TRACKS

Now I want to clarify that I realize there are two tracks at work.

There is the individual contributor (IC) track, and there is the management track. I am not at all saying that one is better than the other. If you want to rise in the ranks as an IC, by all means, keep doing what you are doing. It is working, and by the time you retire, you will be pretty darn happy.

But if you are trying to switch over to an executive leadership position, or you are already an executive but you're doing all the same stuff you did as an IC (and now more), then listen to me and listen closely. Seriously, you have *got to stop doing what you are good at*. I am begging you.

Now, what exactly does that mean? How could you possibly stop doing what you are good at? Isn't that job security? Isn't that WHY you have the job you have? Isn't that why people trust you?

The answer is yes and no. It might be why people trust you as an expert, but it is not why they will trust you to be a leader at your company. It is not why they will trust you to have a seat at the table. It is not why they will trust you to present your ideas to the CEO.

YOU NEED TO STOP DOING ALL OF THIS

Here is what I mean by letting go of what you are good at:

- I mean STOP being so freakin' organized. You have seriously got to stop having conversations with your boss about every little thing on your to-do list. You have got to stop motivating your team through tasks and projects. You need to stop planning your week based on what is on your calendar.
- I mean STOP being so nice. If you are repeatedly told

that you are the nice guy, that is a problem. I know this one oh too well because that was me. If harmony is your number one strength, that is a problem when it comes to being seen as a leader. Now I am not advocating that you be mean instead. I am just saying, stop trying to people-please all the time. Leaders can see right through it, guaranteed.

My client Jennifer, who "never leaves the house without a smile," was actually told by her boss that she was "too nice to be promoted." I probed deeper with her boss during my stakeholder interview, and he revealed that his concern was that she wouldn't be able to have the tough conversations.

So what I coached Jennifer to do was not to stop smiling but simply to be willing to say the hard things. She followed my advice and was a pro at it. Now, not only does her boss not remember giving this feedback, but he would never say that Jennifer couldn't handle the tough conversations. Instead, he has referred to her on multiple occasions as the leader that other executives at their company could learn to emulate.

- I mean STOP relying on your expertise to get ahead. Maybe you have been doing the same thing for fifteen years, and you are really, REALLY good at it. Great. I am so happy for you that you are good at something. But that something is not getting you a seat at the table. In fact, it is keeping you out of the leadership meetings.

Because what they need at the table is someone who can think strategically, and someone who can tie your expertise into the big picture. That someone is not in the weeds all the time doing it all themself.

- I mean STOP meeting deadlines. Okay, you should still totally meet deadlines. But what I mean here is you have got to stop meeting the deadline by yourself. You have got to stop scrambling at the last minute to pull things together. Sometimes that may require extending a deadline. Especially if by doing so you can hit an even bigger target for the organization.

- I mean STOP being a task manager. Just strike that word entirely from your vocabulary. From now on you are going to use words like "strategic" and "vision." You are going to motivate your team through values and ideas and let someone else organize it all. Sound terrifying or impossible? Then that means you especially need to start operating this way.

- I mean STOP being so darn dependable. I have a client who responds to text messages from her boss while she is on a call with me, and she hired me. She paid me good money to be her coach. If she is doing that with me, imagine what she is doing at her job all day. There is nothing that breaks leadership trust more than responding within seconds to every single text. That is bad, bad news.

Another client, a senior vice president of a major retail company, had to train her boss by not responding instantly to his messages. At first she thought this might set him off. He was, after all, a high-stress leader. But with my guidance, she tried it anyway.

It turned out that her boss was relieved that she stopped responding right away. He mentioned that his texts to her were simply to get things off his chest. By her waiting to respond, it allowed him time to reprioritize, and he respected her more as a result. Now she feels more in control of her time, and he views her as a partner—not simply someone who jumps at his every demand.

- I mean STOP relying on your hard work to get ahead. Stop waiting for performance review time to talk about your professional development. STOP thinking that you will just get noticed. I know you "think" it's being respectful, but all it is really doing is showing your boss that you aren't proactive and that you can't think strategically. If you can't speak up for yourself, how are you ever going to be able to lead a team?

You will know you need to let go of what you are good at if you are too organized, too nice, too much of an expert, too reliant on deadlines, too much of a task manager, too dependable, or working too hard.

My question for you is *why?*

I have some ideas. But I think it's important to understand why you are doing things this way.

Is it because you don't know any other way? I get it. How are you supposed to know what else is out there unless you do something different?

Is it because you are too afraid to let go of what's working? Of course you are. If you are like me, and you're in your midforties, it's risky to make such a big career move. People depend on you. You don't have the same energy, drive, or ambition that you had in your twenties. I get it.

Then why do SO MANY managers make this leap into leadership in their forties?

Leadership requires wisdom. Strategic thinking requires someone who has on-the-job experience. How else can they create a vision? Now is actually your time. You know this, or you wouldn't still be reading this right now.

How many hours a week do you spend knowing what you should be doing but not actually doing it?

Think about it. Is it six hours a week? Six hours that you could be taking strategic action? Six hours that you could be networking or meeting people? Six hours that you could be asking better questions and getting to know the leadership team?

Stop wasting your hours!

This all may sound harsh, but I'm telling you this because I truly care about your transformation. There just aren't enough hours in the day. This is not useful for anyone.

Plus, your company needs you to be a leader. Wouldn't it be better for the organization to have you as the senior vice president instead of your coworker who is only out for themself?

Can you do more for your organization?

Think about the trade-offs you are making by being in the weeds all the time.

Think about what brainpower they are missing out on because you aren't able to focus on the big picture and are always putting out fires.

This is ALL possible.

HOW TO GET OUT OF THE WEEDS (AND STAY OUT)
Now, it's time to break down what getting out of the weeds actually looks like in action.

But before we can do that, you need to understand this:

getting out of the weeds is as much about how you are communicating as it is about how you are actually spending your time.

So let's say you don't learn how to delegate better, how to manage your time, or how to prioritize properly. If you simply learn how to communicate better with leadership in a more strategic, visionary way, you're going to begin to get yourself out of the weeds.

WHY GETTING OUT OF THE WEEDS IS NOT ABOUT TIME MANAGEMENT

The first step of getting out of the weeds is to continue to spend your time the exact same way. Don't worry so much about delegating differently or changing the way you organize your time, but instead start communicating differently.

You may think your boss wants to hear all the details and the complete strategy of the project you're working on. Or maybe you think your boss wants to hear about how specific members of your team aren't pulling their own weight, or how you're working on this or that. Perhaps while you're doing all those kinds of updates, you're also complaining a little bit.

You also may think your boss wants to only hear about issues from you once you've already mapped out every single detail.

Wrong!

One piece of really great advice my client received during a stakeholder interview I was conducting was this: "Understand what gets your boss fired. Understand what gets them promoted." That advice always stuck with me.

So this brings me to…

WHAT YOUR BOSS ACTUALLY NEEDS TO KNOW
YOUR OVERALL STRATEGY

It's very simple. *Your boss simply wants to know that you have a strategy.*

A lot of corporate leaders worry that getting out of the weeds will make them look like they aren't doing their jobs, but that's not true. You're shifting to speaking about your job at a much higher level, because your boss really doesn't need to hear all of the details of your entire strategy.

You want to start doing this even if you're still in a middle-management position.

You're going to start shifting the way you're communicating and just say, "I have a strategy in place." Then you could say something like, "If you'd like to hear more details, I'm happy to share them with you."

Don't jump right into the details and spend forty-five minutes talking about them. Because 90 percent of the time, you'll see that they don't want the details anymore. Why? Because by being more strategic, you're building trust.

A student inside of my Executive Ahead of Time program decreased the time spent in her weekly check-ins with her boss from two hours to sixty minutes by using this approach. Not only did she gain more time back in her day to spend on what really matters, but her boss was relieved to have his time back as well.

YOUR OBSTACLES

Remember, your boss doesn't want to hear all about your problems, but they do want to hear about your obstacles. It's very important you don't keep things from your boss, but you want to speak about obstacles as a solution to their problem.

For example, let's say you have a difficult employee or it seems like you're behind on your deadline. Of course, it's still very important that you communicate this to your boss, but you're going to communicate it as the *solution*. You're going to present it as "this is an issue I'm working on" instead of just talking about the problem.

YOU UNDERSTAND THE PROBLEM

This is really, really important. Not only should you ask your boss questions to understand the problem you are trying to solve, but make sure you actually listen for the answer. It sounds simple, but often we ask a question like, "What are your concerns? I was thinking that maybe these things…"

No, stop! Ask the question, "What are your concerns?" and listen to hear their answer.

Here's the kicker: you don't have to solve it right then.

You can say, "Okay, I got it. That makes sense." Or you can ask deeper questions. But just know that you don't have to get defensive and say, "Oh, but I'm working on that." No. You're just listening to them. That is the whole point. You can follow up later. These follow-ups are those check-ins between the meetings.

I interview hundreds of powerhouse leaders on my podcast, and one of the questions I always ask is about their secrets to success. Here is a brilliant response I received from a vice president of engineering of a Fortune 500 company that really illustrates this point.

You'd like to believe you're the smartest person in the room, but you're not as smart as everybody in the room. And so you get a much better result when you're curious about things you don't know. It really does not diminish you at all to ask questions and say, "Hey, I don't know what that means. Can you help me understand?"

Oftentimes what that communicates to the rest of the team is, one, you're confident in yourself and your own abilities, such that you can ask a question and be up front about what you don't know. Two, it helps bring them into the decision-making process; it helps make them feel a part of the whole situation and part of the team.

Which brings me to:

YOU ARE ON IT

This is the most important thing: you're not updating your boss enough. What happens is you want to figure out all the answers ahead of time before you even reach out to your boss. You want to look good, and you want to figure out everything that's coming up.

Here's how to do it.

We've covered that you'll be discussing your overall strategy with your boss during your one-on-one meetings. Now, in between these one-on-ones, you need to update your boss. For example, the day after your one-on-one meeting, you could give them an update like: "From our meeting yesterday, I want you to know that I'm working on these three things." I call this strategy *showing your work.*

So many subject matter experts are very detail-oriented high achievers. They want to wait until they have all the answers, but that's not a core leadership trait.

We don't need to have all of the answers to be at a senior executive level, but we need to communicate a *process* along the way. That's something *you* can begin to do this week.

When you begin speaking to your boss more strategically, you will find that you're also spending your time more strategically.

When I say getting yourself out of the weeds is not about time management, it is and it isn't. When you shift your mindset, the way you're communicating, and how you're preparing for your meetings, *then* you will start spending your time differently. You'll quickly figure out what to let go of and what to delegate.

WHAT SHARING THE VISION INSTEAD OF THE DETAILS LOOKS LIKE

I want you to try this question out. Ask yourself, *How am I going to actually share the vision?*

For example, you could share your vision with your boss by saying something like, "I have really enjoyed working on this project because it aligns with my long-term goal of X, Y, Z."

Or:

"I was thinking more about this project..." and then include what your long-term goal is.

Sometimes I like to tell people to tie it back in. If you're in a larger group meeting, you could say, "When I heard Martha speak earlier, it reminded me of..."

This is what it looks like to be a visionary instead of speaking to the details.

So many of us start with the wrong updates. "These are the problems. This is what I don't understand. I'm not sure what we're going to do." Instead, you want to say what you're confident about and what's working, and then you can ask questions around something else.

Try it. You'll be amazed at how quickly it works. One of my clients who had no resources and no team started implementing these communication strategies, and within weeks, she noticed she had more space in her calendar for strategic thinking.

DELEGATING TO YOUR BOSS

A fun thing I teach my clients is that you can actually delegate to your boss. I want you to understand that. You can tell your boss where you need their support.

One of the ways might be to prioritize. You can ask your boss, "These are the three things I think I need to focus on over the next month. Do you agree?"

You can also ask your boss for resources and other forms of support. You could suggest that your boss run with something at a meeting. Oftentimes, doing this will help you appear very strategic, and it *doesn't* feel like off-loading your responsibility. When you start to do this, you don't even have to worry about whether or not you'll be seen as somebody who doesn't take responsibility for their actions. No. You'll start to be seen as the senior executive leader.

QUESTIONS YOU SHOULD ASK YOUR BOSS

These are some questions I also want to encourage you to ask. Because if you don't have all the answers, you can always ask questions. Questions also make you sound more visionary.

Here they are:

- "What are your expectations for this project?"
- "How frequently should I be checking in with you?"

- "Is there anyone else I should loop in?"
- "What are your concerns?" This is my favorite question. Make sure you understand what matters most to your boss!

I want you to try these communication strategies this week. It's important to put what you're learning into action because that is the fastest way to build confidence in yourself.

You'll *also* notice that people start to treat you differently, and this will help you build even more confidence in yourself.

Just remember that every visionary leader started out this way. Every great leader was once a subject matter expert who turned *themself* into a leader.

CHAPTER SUMMARY

- If the executive team sees you as somebody who can't pull yourself out of the weeds, then you will never get promoted into that next level of leadership. To get out of the weeds, you need to stop doing what you are good at.
- You will know you need to let go of what you are good at if you are too organized, too nice, too much of an expert, too reliant on deadlines, too much of a task manager, too dependable, or working too hard.
- The first step of getting out of the weeds is to start communicating differently. Continue to spend your time the

exact same way. Don't worry so much about delegating differently or changing the way you organize your time, at first.

- This shift in communication starts with no longer jumping into the details during one-on-ones with your boss. The only updates your boss actually needs to know are your overall strategy, your obstacles, and the questions you have. If they want more details, they will ask.
- It's important to understand that even if you think the executives you communicate with only want the details, that's not always the case.

ACTION STEPS

Begin to shift the way you are communicating with your boss.

1. Ask your boss visionary questions. "What are your expectations for this project? How frequently should I be checking in with you? Is there anyone else I should loop in? What are your concerns?"
2. When you have updates, instead of automatically diving into the details, you are going to say this: "If you'd like to hear more details, I'm happy to share them with you."
3. When you bring your obstacles to your boss, make sure to communicate them as a *solution* instead of just talking about the problem. Present your obstacles as "This is an issue I'm working on," and then you can ask if they agree.

4. Show your work by updating your boss more often than you think is necessary. Never let them guess if you are "on it," keeping in mind that updates don't mean going into every little detail.

Download a free guide to asking better questions at stacymayer.com/resources.

CHAPTER 3

STRATEGIC THINKING VS. STRATEGY

By this point, you might be wondering, *OK, Stacy, you want me to let go of doing what I am good at. So what am I going to do instead?*

Exactly! Great question. Because imagine: You start handing off responsibilities to others. You start taking strategic walks during lunchtime. You block an hour a day to think.

Won't your boss think you are shirking your responsibilities? I mean, isn't that what you are most deathly afraid of? Truthfully, it's at the core of why it feels difficult for you to let go of what you are so darn good at doing in the first place.

You have to be aware of what you are going to do instead.

If you are going to give up one thing, you must know what you are going to do instead. This is going to take planning and thought. You have never done it before. You'll have to actually DO something different. You'll have to start becoming the Executive Ahead of Time.

What does becoming the Executive Ahead of Time look like?

It means not reacting to the little problems.

It means painting a vision for your team and your organization.

It means understanding your leadership style and exactly how to communicate that to others.

It means taking your own professional development seriously and making strategic choices about your career so that you not only know where you are headed, but you have a plan to get there.

This applies to you if you've already made it to a vice president role, a senior vice president role, or maybe you are already in the C-suite, but you still feel like you're only getting paid for the hours that you work and not your ideas.

You find yourself constantly jumping in and solving problems for your team or feeling like there's so much more that you can be giving at work, and you're just not able to make that impact.

As a result, you're spinning out. You feel frustrated. You don't know what's next for you.

My client Laura is the vice president of human resources of a major manufacturing company and reports directly to the CEO.

She has a seat at the leadership table. There are only six people in the room. She should have a voice, but when we first started working together, she didn't. She was always being pushed to the last ten minutes of the conversation.

So she said, "Look, I belong at this leadership table, and I've had enough."

I taught her how to start advocating for herself, and how to stop talking about the details all the time. I helped her get really clear on what her actual vision was.

We worked through a step-by-step process that I share in this chapter to get her a stronger voice at the table.

Now she has an incredible relationship with her CEO who runs high-profile ideas by her before they present them to the board.

How good would that feel? To be valued for your ideas and to know that you're making a real impact at your organization?

What if it was actually your job to present ideas, paint a vision, and problem solve on a bigger level?

What if you could do that right now, in the current role with your current title and responsibility?

What if you could take ownership of your career instead of feeling like you were waiting for someone else to tell you that you were good enough?

What if you stopped letting others dictate what you should or should not get done each day, because you were in charge...of it all?

WHAT STRATEGY IS (AND ISN'T)

You now should have a pretty darn good understanding of what it's going to take to actually get yourself out of the weeds. Now we're going to be talking about what you can actually do during your strategic-thinking sessions.

Many people are at a loss when it comes to this. "But how do I actually think more strategically? What should I be planning for? What questions should I be asking myself?" And in this chapter, I'm going to show you.

Before I talk about what to do, let's start with defining what strategic thinking *really* means.

For many of you who are subject matter experts or project managers, you think of strategy as the plan. That's why when you check in with your boss, you're actually saying to them what your plan is. It makes a lot of sense to you. You think that it's strategic, but it's not.

What I'm talking about here is much more visionary. I'm going to teach you about that mindset and what you need to actually be thinking about that's very different from the strategy that you've put together. Strategy usually looks like a series of goals. It can have a nice little timeline, but it's a series of goals and deliverables. It is *not* the process that you're going through.

This chapter was actually inspired by one of my clients during a coaching conversation.

Amir is a senior vice president at a large telecom company in Austin, Texas. His boss repeatedly told him that he was too far in the weeds to be a senior vice president. He was a technical genius, and nobody doubted that. But he was micromanaging his team. He was hovering. He was doing all of the detail work himself. He was working himself to the bone. And his boss, quite frankly, gave him an ultimatum and said, "You need to get yourself out of the weeds. This is not acting like a senior vice president."

So Amir hired a coach (me!). We worked together over several coaching sessions. He was really having a hard time understanding what it was going to look like to start to let go of some of the details. Plus he kept using the word *strategy*. He talked about how he actually does talk to his boss about strategy all of the time. He kept saying, "I'm very strategic!"

Then one day I asked him, "What do you actually say to your boss?" As we went over it together, it became absolutely clear that he was not speaking strategy at all. Instead he was repeatedly getting into the weeds. But to him, it was strategy.

THE ONE THING

This is a quote from *The One Thing*. It's a transformational book and body of work by Gary Keller. Here it is:

> What's the one thing you can do such that by doing it, everything else will be easier or unnecessary?

You should ask yourself this question every single day.

I started this practice about two years ago, and it literally changed everything. What Keller talks about, in essence, is that you can focus on something that takes a very small amount of time but has a huge impact on your workload. It's like the domino effect, right? If you just get all of these pieces lined up, all you have to do is push that one domino, and then everything else becomes easier or completely unnecessary. Start asking yourself this every day. Did this get me closer to my goal? Did I pick the easiest thing?

When you're thinking about career advancement, so many of us are focusing on turning our boss around. But it's possible that all you need to do is have *one* conversation with *one* senior executive, and then your whole promotion process becomes that much easier.

HOW TO FIND YOUR CORE PILLARS

Knowing how to pull yourself out of the weeds as well as trusting that you can lead at a higher executive level is a huge indicator of your success.

To do this, you need to understand the core pillars to share with your boss so you can focus on the project instead of all the details. These are the things they *actually* need to know, and you'll do that by asking yourself two powerful questions.

WHAT IS THE PROBLEM YOU ARE TRYING TO SOLVE?

This is really, really easy for most people. What is the problem you're trying to solve right now?

I want you to take that problem and turn it into a powerful vision statement.

For example, let's say you are a human resources professional, and your main problem is retention. You might be thinking about how to get people to stay because people are leaving too quickly. You noticed that millennials in particular don't have enough longevity at your company. How do you turn this problem into a powerful vision statement?

You say, "Our goal is to have a company where even millennials want to stay for ten or twenty years and retire here."

HOW DOES THIS TIE INTO WHAT THE ORGANIZATION IS TRYING TO ACCOMPLISH RIGHT NOW?

It's important that you really understand the organization's goals and how your project ties into those goals.

Ask yourself, *What are the main areas of focus that I'm going to concentrate on over the next six months, and how do these tie into the organization's goals?*

THE THREE THINGS LEADERSHIP ACTUALLY WANTS TO HEAR FROM YOU

No, your boss doesn't need all the details. In fact, they don't want them. Here are the three things your boss *actually* needs to hear from you:

1. **Project Updates.** They don't need to hear all the details

of your project. They just need to know the status of the project. So simply tell them where you are in the process.

2. **Problems.** The second thing your boss needs to know is if you have any problems. And I *always* suggest that when you tell your boss your problem, you offer a solution as well. That way you're not bringing them problems to solve all the time, but you're still updating them on your obstacles and what you're working on.

3. **What You Need.** One of the most important things you can tell your boss is simply what you need from them, and you need to say it out loud. Maybe you need them to follow up on an email you sent several days earlier. Or maybe you need them to introduce you to somebody. Or perhaps you need them to talk to somebody on your team. Whatever it is, be sure to let your boss know specifically what you need from them.

ASK YOURSELF THIS BEFORE EVERY MEETING

Here is the most important question you can ask yourself before every single meeting: *What do I want the outcome to be?*

For example, let's say you're going into a big leadership team meeting. In that case, perhaps an outcome you would want would be that you speak before you're ready. That's it. Super simple. If you're somebody who waits until they have all the answers, until they know exactly what they're going to say before they actually speak up, maybe your goal is to speak up a little bit sooner.

It can really be that simple.

A CASE STUDY ON THE POWER OF BEING VISIONARY

I want to paint you a picture of what being strategic and being called to that next level of leadership looks like in action.

This happened to a client of mine, Yolanda.

She was working on a project that was very high profile with the leadership team. In fact, it was a crisis at the time for the organization.

Here's what happened. When the opportunity to work on this project came up, my client was completely overwhelmed.

Yolanda was working sixty hours a week, and she oversaw almost 200 people. She knew she didn't really have a lot of extra time, but this project was inspiring to her, and she knew she could make a big impact.

Plus, it was an opportunity to get in front of the leadership team and be seen as a decision maker in this initiative. So

I coached her through the process as she worked on the project.

It wasn't long before the leadership team began to call on her to discuss this crisis.

And why is that?

Because she had already proven that she was *willing*—not only willing to go to bat for the organization to begin with, but that she had strong ideas.

Of course, Yolanda's still working sixty-hour weeks, but her work is more impactful. She knows she is making a difference. She knows her opinion and her voice matter, and the leadership team respects her for that. They're asking for her opinion.

The only reason she is able to do that now is because she built that trust as a strategic leader.

That is what I am calling on YOU to do. Ask yourself, *How can I start to build that trust at that higher leadership level?*

This doesn't happen from doing all the things. It comes from thinking like a visionary and having a strategic vision for your team.

CHAPTER SUMMARY

- Becoming the Executive Ahead of Time means painting a vision for your team/organization, understanding your leadership style and how to communicate it, taking your own professional development seriously, having a plan to get to the next level, and no longer reacting to the little problems. It does not mean having all the answers.

- Knowing how to pull yourself out of the weeds, as well as trusting that you can lead at a higher executive level, is a huge indicator of whether or not you will be promoted.

- The three things leadership actually wants to hear from you are project updates, any problems you may be experiencing, and what you need from them. To do this, you'll want to understand the core pillars that you need to share with your boss so you can focus on the project instead of all the details.

- You will do that by asking yourself two powerful questions: *What is the problem you are trying to solve?* and *How does this tie into what the organization is trying to accomplish right now?*

- To help you think more strategically, ask yourself this question before every meeting: *What do I want the outcome to be?*

ACTION STEPS

Knowing how to pull yourself out of the weeds as well as trusting that you can lead at a higher executive level is a huge indicator of your success. To do this, you must understand the core pillars that you need to share with your boss so you can focus on the project instead of all the details.

Ask yourself the following two powerful questions to discover your core pillars.

WHAT IS THE PROBLEM YOU ARE TRYING TO SOLVE?

To properly answer this question, you must:

Step 1: Identify the problem.

Step 2: Turn the problem into a powerful vision statement.

For example, let's say you are a human resources professional, and your main problem is retention. You might be thinking about how to get people to stay because people are leaving too quickly. You noticed that millennials in particular don't have enough longevity at your company. How do you turn this problem into a powerful vision statement? You say, "Our goal is to have a company where even millennials want to stay for ten or twenty years and retire here."

HOW DOES THIS TIE INTO WHAT THE ORGANIZATION IS TRYING TO ACCOMPLISH RIGHT NOW?

It's important that you really understand the organization's goals and how your project ties into those goals. Ask yourself, *What are the main areas of focus that I'm going to concentrate on over the next six months, and how do these tie into the organization's goals?*

SET A DESIRED OUTCOME FOR EVERY MEETING

Ask yourself, *What do I want the outcome to be?*

For example, let's say you're going into a big leadership team meeting. Your outcome could be that you want to build trust with the other executives in the meeting.

Download free resource guides at stacymayer.com/resources.

CHAPTER 4

THE CASE FOR 3×ING YOUR CAREER VISION

The right time and the right place isn't something that just happens to you. It is something you create.

To do this, you must have a clear vision for your career first.

You know that having a clear vision is important, but the majority of corporate leaders I meet are so far into the weeds that they don't feel they have time to create a clear vision for themself.

I regularly conduct stakeholder interviews for my clients. One day I was interviewing a powerhouse chief technology officer for a major manufacturing company, and she described the lack of career vision like this:

Stacy, you would be amazed at the number of leaders who don't have a response when I ask them what they want. Instead, they say they'll get back to me, or they tell me something wishy-washy or unclear.

Still, even having a clear vision can only get you so far. That's why I teach my clients to 3× the vision for their career instead.

Many of my clients, when they first come to me, are thinking too small. They are making decisions and having conversations about what it is going to take to get them to that next promotion. Since they are solely focused on that next level, some of the decisions they are making are really bad decisions.

You won't find this advice in any other leadership book, but I've been using this strategy to get client after client promoted into senior leadership positions, and it works.

First, you must understand what a 3× Vision for your career really is. The simplest way to think about it is that it's not your next role or the role after that—it's the role you want to be at three promotion cycles from now.

It works like this. Let's say you're at a director level and you want to be promoted to a senior director position.

You've been talking to your boss about becoming a senior

director. They've helped you map out a plan. But…it seems like it's taking a little bit longer than you would like. You're not really sure when it's going to happen. In the meantime, you're just doing your work, and you're starting to feel a little bit frustrated.

But how would things change if you got really clear on what your 3× Vision was?

What would happen if you didn't focus on becoming a senior director or even a vice president, but you focused on what it would take to become a senior vice president? What decisions are you making today that you would not make if you were a senior vice president?

HOW YOUR 3× VISION WORKS

With a 3× Vision, the first step is to simply admit that it's possible, and then take action toward reaching that vision. Here's how it works.

When we 3× our vision, we take different, bolder action steps. That's because we're not focused on the *next* role. No. If you want to be in the C-suite, you need to start acting like an executive now.

Your 3× Vision will show you how to prioritize. It will help you get out of the weeds. It's going to clarify what the leadership team needs to see from you. *That* is how you start becoming the executive leader long before the promotion happens.

WHY IT'S SO IMPORTANT TO 3× YOUR CAREER VISION

You are a high performer. You probably have to set goals for your team all the time. You know how to measure these goals. You probably have pretty good ideas for your career as well. That's nothing new.

The challenge that I see a lot of managers facing is that they're not getting the recognition they deserve. They're not having the impact they want at work. They're not being invited to the leadership table. They're being passed over for promotions.

All because they aren't thinking big enough about their careers.

So I want to challenge you to start thinking about what your vision would look like if you stepped it up three notches.

Now, the interesting thing is that it's actually very difficult to do. The reason for that is because you're thinking about goals in the wrong way. Here's what I mean. You're thinking about a goal as something that you know exactly how to achieve. This is important, so I'm going to repeat it. You're thinking about your goals as something *practical.* You know exactly how you are going to achieve them.

We usually accomplish these kinds of goals because they're very small in the first place. We might be willing to say, "Oh, it would be nice to be that next level up," but when you say, "I want to be a CFO someday," it feels too far ahead of you.

I want you to flip that. I want you to start to think about goals as more of a vision, as a direction to head in, as a thing with which to measure every single action you take in your life. To always be asking yourself, *Will this thing that I'm doing today get me closer to my long-term vision?* This kind of clarity is going to show you how to prioritize, how to focus on what's important, and how to be more productive. It's the most important thing that's going to give you the biggest return on your investment.

When you know your long-term goals, and you're stretching yourself beyond what you actually think is possible, you are challenging yourself in a way that gets you out of the practical and out of your head. Oftentimes when we're stuck in our head and we're stuck in the "How is this actually going to play out?" then we can't achieve our goals.

Now back to my client Diana, who I mentioned in the introduction. She was a director of finance when we first started working together.

Diana knew she wanted to be a vice president. That was her next level up. But really, what she wanted was to be a CFO someday. I asked her how long she thought it would take for her to become a CFO. She answered, "At least five to ten years."

So I challenged her and said, "Okay. Well, what if it doesn't happen in five years? What if it happened in three?"

Her response? "Well, I have to change a lot of things if I want to become CFO in three years!" That's when we got to work on changing those things.

Setting that 3x goal made us start to discuss all the things she would need to change if she wanted to become CFO in three years instead of five years. She made decisions about how she was spending her time. She strengthened her relationship with her boss. And she developed the courage to have a few difficult conversations with her peers.

That's what I mean by 3xing your vision for your career. For Diana, it meant taking it up a notch. She still has to become vice president before she can become CFO, but now the vice president position seems totally attainable because really, she's shooting to become CFO. So you're starting to see, I hope, how this works a little bit.

Now, I want to tell you the magic of the story.

We got to work on Diana's vision. She made some really big decisions in her career. She got out of the weeds. She really focused on what that higher-level leadership position would look like, how she would have to manage and prioritize her time so she could spend time with her family, and really, how to focus on the most important thing so she wasn't just working herself into a hole.

So we focused on all of those things. We changed that in real time. Then they announced layoffs in her department.

It was clear that she would be laid off within the next six months. But because she was so clear and she was already performing at the vice president level, she went out and found a vice president role within just three weeks.

And guess what? When she interviewed for that job, she shared with them her 3× Vision. She literally told them, "I want to be a CFO someday." She was super clear. So it was a no-brainer for them to hire her as vice president because they wanted her to become CFO as well. They just didn't need a CFO yet, but…within ten months of having that job, she did in fact become their CFO. So instead of it taking five to ten years to reach her goal, she did it in less than two years.

That is the power of 3×ing your vision. It can happen quickly, and it can happen in your favor. But you have to actually make it happen. This is why it's so important to think bigger.

When you 3× your vision, you naturally start to act like you're already in that next-level role because you're thinking so much further ahead. You essentially start acting like the vice president now before you've actually been given the title.

And acting like the vice president before you have a vice president position doesn't just show the leadership team that you want the role, it allows them to trust that you can actually do the job when you get there.

So I encourage you to take a moment and brainstorm the behaviors you would need to start doing now in order to go one level up. How can you, metaphorically, start "dressing" for the job you want, versus the job you already have?

BUT I DON'T REALLY WANT TO BE IN THE C-SUITE SOMEDAY

Often I meet leaders who never really focused on making it to the C-suite someday. It's not a thing they wanted to do. They just wanted to be good at their job.

Does this sound like you?

You get great performance reviews. People look up to you. Your team likes you.

Yet when you have check-ins with your boss, you're still very detail-oriented. You're basically going through a scorecard, and you feel like every time you're in front of the executive team, all they ask you about is what you're working on. They ask you about the details.

This is fine because you always wanted to be the expert in your field and you really love that. But then, at the end of the day, it still feels a little empty. It feels like you should be further along by now. "I should be getting paid for my ideas. I wish somebody would actually ask me for my opinion."

Even worse is that people are passing you up so that people who are less qualified than you, worse leaders than you, are getting promoted. So you're getting passed over for promotion after promotion, and you feel a little bit fed up.

This is the exact description of my client Christine.

Christine is a technology director at a Fortune 500 company. She joined my Executive Ahead of Time because she felt stuck.

She said, "I've been a director of engineering for a while. People are passing me up for promotions. I never really thought about what I wanted in my career. I do see myself as a subject matter expert. That doesn't seem to bother me that much. I like being good at my job, but maybe I could be doing something more?"

I realized quickly that she was thinking too small. So I taught her to become a corporate badass by 3×ing her vision.

Having her 3× Vision meant that she was now super clear on exactly where she wanted to go in her career. And since she now knows where she is going, it's much easier for her to make the right decisions at work every single day.

But it took time. She actually wrote fifteen versions of her 3× Vision over the course of the program. That was the work she needed to do. She needed to challenge herself and get super clear. And it showed her what to do next.

BREAKING YOUR 3× VISION DOWN INTO ACTION STEPS

You've heard of SMART goals, right? It's the belief that goals need to be specific, measurable, actionable, results-oriented, and time-bound. This isn't something I teach very often to my clients (I have a preferred method that I share in Chapter 9), but I get that we need to have goals that we can attain.

The way I think about goals is that our vision is a longer vision, and then we break it down into the action steps. How are we actually going to get to that vision? That's where practicality comes in. That's when it can become short term.

So you can say, "I want to become CFO someday." What you're actually going to do is start acting like the vice president. So what are the ways you can start acting like the vice president today? Because if you want to become CFO, you have to understand what the role of a vice president is like, right? You're going to ask yourself these questions and make these changes, all while keeping in mind what that longer vision for your career looks like.

WHY YOU'RE RESISTANT TO 3×ING YOUR CAREER VISION

One of the reasons why you might be hesitant to 3× the vision for your career is because you don't understand what that actual career path would entail.

Let's say you have some really bad role models at the top of your organization. Maybe they work themselves to the bone, they spend no time with their families, they're frustrated all the time, they micromanage their teams, and they're always making harsh, fast decisions that seem to benefit no one. They seem like they're always worried about their job security, and they're stressed out all the time. When we have somebody like that who is above us, it's really easy to not want their job. You don't want to be like that.

Executives often end up in that position because they scaled their bad habits with them. They're still in the weeds, they have a poor network, or they're still not thinking strategically.

You don't have to be like them. The way that you stop

yourself from being like them is to start thinking more strategically now. Start thinking long term, start getting out of the weeds, and start grooming your successor.

Another reason why so many managers are hesitant to really own this bigger, more aspirational vision for their career is because of the organization or the leadership team they currently work for.

Let's say that you've been working for your company for fifteen years and you've noticed that the promotion process is very slow. In fact, you need to be in a position for at least three years before you can hope for a promotion.

Or you look at the current executive team and realize that there is a lack of diversity or inclusiveness. The last thing you want to do is be in a position of power at an organization that doesn't share your same values. So you're using the limitations of your specific organization and your specific situation to limit you from even setting the goal.

What I want to do is challenge you to set the goal and figure out how you're going to get there afterward. How do we do that? It starts with visualization.

USING VISUALIZATIONS TO ACHIEVE YOUR GOALS

Elon Musk has a goal to travel to Mars. As a result, every

decision he makes (from Tesla to SpaceX) is aligned with that goal and whether or not that decision will get him closer to being able to land people on Mars.

I want *you* to do the same. Not in terms of going to Mars (of course!), but I want you to align every decision you're making about your career to ensure it is getting you to where you want to go. By decisions, I mean how you're showing up at work every day, how you're taking care of your body, how you're taking care of your health, and how you're staying focused on the bigger picture. Do you have the networks you need? Do you have the right sponsors and mentors? Are you getting the support that you need?

So my challenge to you this week is I want you to take it up a notch. I want you to think bigger. I want you to stop worrying about how you're going to get there and just create the vision for yourself. Make yourself laugh a little bit and remind yourself of what it was like when you were twenty years old and you felt like you could do anything. To say to yourself, "This is what I want. You know why I want it? It's because I'm good at it." I want you to write that on a Post-it note and stick it on your computer. Then say, "I want to be CFO someday because I'm good at it." "I want to be chief operations officer because I'm good at it." "I want to be the vice president of marketing because I'm good at it."

Then go and figure out all the reasons why you're so great at it and start doing them today. I guarantee if you start acting like you're in the role that you want now, you're going to get it sooner and faster—and you're going to be better at the job once you actually get there.

Now you might be thinking, *I can't do that, Stacy! My job is so different than it would be if I was in a senior vice president position.*

I get it. But there are *some* action steps you could start taking today to set yourself up to become that senior vice president someday. When you base your decisions on your 3× Vision, everything else falls into place. The meetings you're attending, the way you're communicating with your boss, the people in your network, the people you're communicating with—all these decisions are based on that 3× Vision.

When you start to make decisions from your 3× Vision, you're going to feel empowered. You're going to feel strong. You're going to feel motivated. You're also going to put some pieces into place.

CHAPTER SUMMARY

- 3×ing your vision for your career means that you are deciding where you want to be in your career three promotions from now.
- If you want to be in a senior executive leadership posi-

tion, you need to become the executive leader ahead of time. Your 3× Vision will show you how to prioritize. It will help you get out of the weeds. It's going to clarify what the leadership team needs to see from you.

- Becoming the vice president before you have a vice president position doesn't just show the leadership team that you want the role. It allows them to trust that you can actually do the job when you get there.
- Brainstorm the behaviors you would need to start doing now in order to go one level up. How can you, metaphorically, start "dressing" for the job you want, versus the job you already have?
- The meetings you're attending, the way you're communicating with your boss, the people in your network, the people you're communicating with—all these decisions are based on that 3× Vision.

CHAPTER 5

DEFINING YOUR LEADERSHIP STYLE

You've likely heard of this concept before: what got you here won't get you there. It's also the title of a fantastic book by Marshall Goldsmith.

What this means in terms of your career is what got you here is being the subject matter expert (your attention to detail, your knowledge of every single thing that's going on). But what is going to get you *there* is leading a team, inspiring action, creating change, coming up with outside-of-the-box ideas, and innovative thinking. *That* is what gets you to that next level of leadership.

Your subject matter expertise got you here. Now to get to that next level, you need to step into leadership.

BELIEVE YOU CAN BECOME A SENIOR EXECUTIVE LEADER

Scaling your career when you're known as the subject matter expert is difficult, if not next to impossible. Not simply because of how other people see you, but because of how you view yourself.

I don't care if you're a senior manager, a director, or a senior vice president. If you identify with having all of the answers, your thinking is not scalable. It makes it really difficult for you to trust yourself to lead at a higher executive level. That is why it is imperative to understand your own unique leadership style.

You must first understand and trust that you are a great manager. We know this already. You are a brilliant subject matter expert. You're really great at what you do. I also want you to know that you deserve a senior executive leadership position. If you want to become an executive leader, you need to believe that you are capable of being a senior executive leader.

You need to get clear on why you're an incredible LEADER first.

Answer these questions for yourself: What is your leadership style? How do you identify yourself? Why are you an amazing manager? Why do they need you in a senior executive leadership role (because they do!)?

The answer cannot just be because of your depth of knowledge and your subject matter expertise. Your value to your organization is not just because you've been there for eighteen years. So begin to understand where your leadership value comes from instead.

What it takes to get promoted into a senior executive leadership position is trust that you can do the job at a higher executive level. And that trust starts with trusting yourself.

Now, you might be somebody who's been trying to get a promotion for a while, and you're thinking to yourself, *Of course, Stacy. I know I'm fully capable. I've been thinking about this for a very long time, and I've been trying to show them.*

But here's the thing. You don't *actually* believe it, right? There's still something blocking you.

Even if you're going for that higher-level leadership position, you may still be relying on your expert mentality that we talked about in Chapter 2, right? That you get paid by the hours that you work and by the time that you put into your job. The truth is, your value is in your *ideas*. That's what they need at the senior executive level.

I also want to show you how to differentiate yourself. Once you believe and really understand your own unique leadership style, and you know what it's going to take to get you into that senior executive leadership position, you can begin to share that with other people.

The fastest way to build trust with leadership is to trust yourself first. Trust that you are fully capable of leading at a senior executive level. Trust that you can make decisions at that higher executive level. Trust that you have what it takes to be resourceful and not to have all the answers, but to go out and find the answers.

We do that by defining our leadership style.

DEFINE YOUR LEADERSHIP STYLE

Now, it's important to note that your leadership style doesn't actually change from the time that you started out as a leader. When you were twelve years old, and you were in Girl Scouts, all the way until you got your first people management role, or even landed a position at the C-suite level, your leadership style is something that usually stays.

Your leadership style is unique to you and is different from your personality assessment, your strengths, and your values. It's actually a combination of all of the above. It's what you believe in as a leader. It's what you respect and admire in other people. It's what you aspire to do. It is, in fact, rooted in your values system because it's something that you care deeply about. It's something that you can really excel at. It's something that makes you great. Your leadership style is the "why" behind why you became a leader.

There are three main reasons why understanding your leadership style is so important.

#1: IT HELPS KEEP YOU MOTIVATED

At certain times in your career, you might feel less than inspired, less than recognized, less than supported by your team, and feeling like you have too much work to do. So, you might start to ask yourself, *Why do I put in so much time and effort and get so few rewards?*

This can be super frustrating, but understanding your leadership style and being able to articulate your hard "why" for yourself is so important in getting you back out of the funk.

#2: IT'S IMPORTANT TO BE ABLE TO ARTICULATE YOUR LEADERSHIP STYLE TO OTHERS

I created a leadership style assessment that I offer in my coaching programs because it can give you really concrete language to be able to speak about what it is that you do really, really well. When you can articulate that both to yourself and to other people, it helps them to communicate with you better. It helps you to better communicate with them. It also lets you see where some of your blind spots might be.

#3: ONCE YOU'RE ABLE TO ARTICULATE YOUR LEADERSHIP STYLE TO PEOPLE, THEN YOU CAN FIGURE OUT WHERE THE BEST MATCHES ARE FOR YOU

This will help you say yes to certain projects and no to the ones that aren't aligned with your long-term vision. You're going to be able to confidently ask for more responsibility, and you can do it in a way that's really authentic and genuine to what it is that you actually care about in the organization.

Here's an exercise I want to walk you through. First, grab a pen and paper.

Next, I want you to take ten minutes and journal about a time in your career where leadership just felt effortless, a time when it felt really good and things just worked out. Think of one single story. Set a timer for ten minutes and just write it down.

What do you remember about that time? What were you doing? What made you successful? What were the people like around you? What was your morning like? How did you manage your time back then? What were all of the things you were doing at that time in your life that made you successful as a leader?

Once you're done, I want you to go back through your notes and identify three key reasons why you had that success.

Circle it, point to it, mindmap it, whatever you prefer. Just really identify why.

Was it because you were collaborative? Was it because people respected you? What were those key areas that stood out to you?

Then I want you to think about what you, personally, were the proudest of at that time. What made you just feel so good inside? When you look back at that story, why do you feel really great about that time?

Finally, you're going to turn that into a two- to three-word description, and we're going to start to call that your leadership style.

This exercise is based on the process of Appreciative Inquiry, a psychological approach to creating change by focusing on past experiences. Meaning: we've created a result in the past, which means we can do it again in the future. It's a methodology that tells our brain that things are possible. That's what we're starting to do. We're starting to tell ourselves that we actually do deserve to be a CFO. That we have the capability to be a CFO because past situations prove it. Because similar characteristics are going to be required of us at that senior executive level. You know how to do it.

Now I'm going to share with you some actual results from

the leadership style assessments that I do with my clients. As you're reading these, I want you to identify for yourself what qualities you think you really emulate as a leader already. Not what you want or wish you could be, but the type of leader you are today without changing anything.

What matters to you? What resonates with you when I'm giving you these examples? What gets you excited? What makes you say, "Oh yeah, that's me," or "Oh yeah, that's my mentor."

LEADERSHIP STYLE EXAMPLES

THE HUMBLE LEADER

The humble leader is someone who is willing to get in and get their hands dirty. They want to know the actual issues. They're okay with not having all the answers and are willing to ask questions and to listen. They value working as a team and not being the sole leader on a particular project.

THE VISIONARY LEADER

The visionary leader is hands off on the actual steps and the process that it will take to get there, but they are willing to create the vision for their team and use opportunities to learn, grow, and think bigger. They believe in the power of people and the possibility of "what comes next."

THE SENSITIVE LEADER

The sensitive leader is someone who's extremely well-rounded. They're intuitive and can pick up on other people's needs and see things before they become actual problems. They understand the energy of the room and know how to capture it or call out the elephant in the room.

THE RESULTS-DRIVEN LEADER

The results-driven leader is someone who is very invested in the ROI. They have a super linear focus. They may ask questions like, "How are we going to do the steps in this process? How are we going to get there? Is this actually going to work?" They value open communication and like to gather information. They want to make sure they have a pulse on every step of the way so they can make sure they know every single thing that's happening.

THE HIGH-PERFORMANCE LEADER

The high-performance leader is someone who is willing to make tough decisions, to get dirty, to work really, really hard, but also to think about the big picture. They are the leader who knows how to take care of their health and to support themself so they can ask for what they need.

THE IMPACTFUL LEADER

The impactful leader is someone who is super focused on how something is impacting the people on the team or the organization. They want to understand how their actions are impacting the organization.

THE RESPONSIBLE LEADER

The responsible leader never drops the ball. This leader respects collaboration and is always focused on the bottom line. They make sure their boss is up to date every single step of the way. If you ask them to do something, it is 150 percent going to get done. This leader is extremely resourceful and knows how to work hard.

THE COLLABORATIVE LEADER

The collaborative leader is someone who is not worried about getting credit. This leader wants to make sure that it's a group effort.

THE SELF-MADE LEADER

The self-made leader is someone who has all the odds stacked against them, but they made their own way. They're the person who came to the leadership table from the mail room. Not because of their MBA, but because of their values, because they strive for more, and because they always push themself to do better.

THE TRANSPARENT LEADER

The transparent leader is someone who wants to be a constant role model for others. This type of leader tends to mentor other people and wants to make sure that they're always showing up in a true and authentic way.

THE BROAD-VIEW LEADER

The broad-view leader is the person who is able to see perspective and think in a bigger way. They notice problems that other people don't notice. They're the leader who's willing to ask for feedback because they are able to look at the bigger picture and not get caught up in a particular situation.

You might have read all of these qualities and thought to yourself, *Well, aren't these all just the signs of good leadership?* And yes, they are. They're all really incredible leadership qualities. Every single one of them.

But if you go back through this chapter, you'll notice that there are very subtle differences between each and every one.

It's important to understand that subtlety. We get mixed up

a lot in what we're supposed to be doing, and what we think a good leader looks like. But this is an opportunity for you to get super honest with yourself. What is it that matters most to you about leadership? What is going to drive you, and what is going to motivate you as you continue to rise in your corporate career?

This is important because as we continue to rise, and as we get closer and closer to the top, the lonelier it gets. The only person who you're left with is yourself. And if you don't love yourself and understand what motivates and inspires you and brings you joy, then it's going to be really difficult to be happy at the end of the day. In fact, it's going to be even harder to push yourself to grow and to continue learning and investing in your professional development.

These are just examples of leadership styles. I encourage you to take what is here and make it your own. Go back to your paper and claim your own unique leadership style.

I promise you, if you get super clear on your leadership style, learn how to start communicating that with others, and see what other people's leadership styles are, then you will have more enjoyment. You will feel more passionate at your job, and you will be able to make the impact that you really want to be making at your organization.

HOW TO PUT YOUR LEADERSHIP STYLE TO USE

The next thing I want you to understand is that you already have these leadership skills, but you might not be using them right. You might need to elevate them a little bit.

Take the skills that have made you successful in the past and start to use them even more now. It's the best place to start. Let's start with what's actually working rather than trying to fix what's broken. Of course, you're going to fix your delegation skills, and you're going to fix your time management problems. But what I want you to think about is if you're a resourceful leader. If that is what you identified above, then do more of that. Be even more resourceful and start sharing your process with other people.

When you're having conversations with your boss, you're going to talk about how you were resourceful. You're going to point to those things, because it's just going to be really easy. That's what you've already been doing. You're a great manager. I want you to start to see that you are already doing essentially high-performance leadership skills.

I want you to create a weekly practice of evaluating and asking yourself, *Am I still doing this? Am I being a resourceful leader this week, or am I in the weeds all the time?*

WHAT THE LEADERSHIP TEAM IS LOOKING FOR IN YOU

So now you understand that you already have the leadership abilities to succeed at that higher executive level. Now I want you to understand what the leadership team is looking at you to do.

There are core management skills that you are really, really great at already—skills like data analysis, technical aptitude, institutional knowledge, organization, troubleshooting, reliability, and leadership.

Now, I want you to take these core management skills and turn them into leadership traits.

You're not necessarily changing what you're doing on a regular basis. You're changing how you think about yourself on a regular basis.

For example, are you productive? You might be very organized, but are you productive? Do you know how to focus on the most important problems? Are you a decision maker? Do you know how to discern? Do you know what you need to say to the leadership versus your own team? Do you know how to use people's time wisely? Are you very deliberate in your actions? Are you resourceful? Do you know and take pride in maintaining your energy? Are you putting yourself out there? Are you being courageous? Are you raising your hand?

These are all core leadership traits. Some of them will overlap with core management skills, but they're called something slightly different.

Think about where your skills already overlap, because you are already a great manager. Now it's time to show everyone that you are also an extraordinary leader.

CHAPTER SUMMARY

- What got you *here* is being the subject matter expert. But what is going to get you *there* is leading a team, inspiring action, creating change, and being innovative.
- You need to get clear on why you're an incredible leader already. Identify your unique leadership style. How do you identify yourself? Why are you an amazing manager? Why do they need you in a senior executive leadership role (because they do!)?
- The fastest way to build trust with leadership is to trust yourself first. Trust that you are fully capable of leading and making decisions at a senior executive level. We do that by defining our leadership style.
- There are three reasons why understanding your leadership style is important. 1) It helps keep you motivated; 2) It's important to be able to articulate your leadership style to others; and 3) Once you're able to articulate your leadership style to executives, then you can also articulate where the best matches are for you.

- Create a weekly practice of evaluating and asking yourself, *Am I still using my unique leadership style to guide my decisions and actions?*

ACTION STEPS

IDENTIFY YOUR CORE LEADERSHIP STYLE

1. Take ten minutes and journal about a time in your career where leadership felt effortless, a time when it felt really good and things just worked out. Think of one single story. Questions to ask yourself: *What do you remember about that time? What were you doing? What made you successful? What were the people like around you? What was your morning like? How did you manage your time back then? What were all of the things that you were doing at that time in your life that made you successful as a leader?*

2. Refer to your notes and identify three key reasons why you had that success. For example: *Was it because you were collaborative? Was it because people respected you? What were those key areas that stood out to you?*

3. Then I want you to think about what you were the proudest of at that time. Questions to ask yourself: *What made you just feel so good inside? When you look back at that story, why do you feel really great about that time?*

4. Finally, you're going to turn that into a two- to three-word description, and we're going to start to call that your leadership style.

PUT YOUR LEADERSHIP STYLE TO USE

Take the leadership traits you've identified above, and use more of them. Communicate these traits by sharing your process with people. For example, if one of your core leadership traits is resourcefulness, you could talk about how you were resourceful the next time you are having a one-on-one conversation with your boss.

Download a free leadership style assessment at stacymayer.com/resources.

CHAPTER 6

BUILD TRUST WITH 15-MINUTE ALLY MEETINGS

Throughout this book, I've shown you how to pull yourself out of the weeds so you can tap into strategic thinking (that part of your brain that can see the bigger vision and really understand leadership at a higher executive level).

We've talked about 3×ing your vision for your career and how you can begin to make decisions accordingly.

You've learned how to build trust within yourself, but it's a whole different story to show the executives that you are ready to lead at a higher level. In this chapter, I'll show you the fastest way to do it.

THE TWO DEFINITIONS OF TRUST

When I was growing up, my mom used to tell me that trust was *everything*. She always reminded me that if someone trusted me, I needed to make sure that I never broke that trust. According to her, it was the hardest thing in the world to repair.

She instilled this belief in me from a very young age. She also taught me how to trust *her*. We used to make a lot of pinky promises together to show that we could trust each other.

This brings me to *you*.

You don't have problems with that sort of trust. You're an excellent manager. You work really hard. You always meet your deadlines. You go above and beyond expectations. This is showing up for you on a regular basis on your performance review. You're getting decent reviews. You're an excellent subject matter expert. You're always applauded for your effort. This is that kind of trust.

But the trust that I'm going to be talking about in this chapter is a little bit different.

It isn't trusting you can deliver on your results—you've proven that. This is trust that you have the ability to lead at a higher executive level. This is the type of trust that really stumps people who are having difficulty getting promoted into senior-level executive roles. It feels almost impossible to figure out how to build that trust.

Now, this is super important for very obvious reasons, but the main reason is because we want other people to advocate on your behalf. It is a lot of work to both do your job and continue to promote yourself *and* promote your own professional development. We need to get other people to work with and advocate for us to really advance in our careers.

As you know, this is often easier said than done. That's why it's important to think about advocating for a promotion as building trust with leadership and letting them know that you're ready to lead at a higher executive level.

When it comes to letting leadership know about your career ambitions, you want to make sure that it's not a yes/no question. This is also the beauty of the 3× Vision because it allows you to speak up in a way that's not a yes or no answer. Here's what I mean.

If you're having a conversation with your boss and you're constantly saying, "I want to be promoted to a senior director, I want to be promoted to a senior director, I want to be promoted to a senior director," they're just answering you with yes or no, right?

They might say it's not the right time, or that it *might* happen during this promotion cycle. But the conversation that's much more useful to have with your boss is the one about your 3× Vision.

Instead of asking about becoming a senior director, you're telling your boss, "I want to become a senior vice president someday. What's it going to take to get there?"

NOW you're showing them that you're ready for growth. You're actually advocating for yourself in a way that shows them you're here, you're in it for the long haul, and you want to grow with your organization. You want to do bigger, badder, bolder things.

TRUSTING IN YOURSELF THAT YOU CAN LEAD AT THAT HIGHER EXECUTIVE LEVEL

"We ask ourselves, who am I to be brilliant, gorgeous, talented, fabulous? Actually, who are you not to be?"

—MARIANNE WILLIAMSON

I know if you're reading this book that you want to be recognized. You want to do more at your organization, and you're ready to take your leadership to that next level. But do you really trust yourself?

The reason I'm asking this question so boldly is because part of you doesn't trust yourself. Part of you doesn't trust that you can lead at that higher executive level.

Let's just get real with ourselves right now. Let's ask ourselves, *Do I trust that I can lead at that higher executive level?* Notice where the gaps are. Notice where your identity falls short.

Here's what I mean. You may be thinking, *Well, I can lead as long as I'm doing these things.*

Those "things" are often the things that you find yourself complaining about. Like, "Every time I have a meeting with my boss, I'm always in the weeds, and I don't really know how to get out of them."

If you feel this way, it's a sign that you don't trust your ability to speak more to the strategy. You know that if you're going to lead at that higher executive level, then you're going to have to think strategically.

So I want you to start noticing and questioning, *Where does my trust in myself fall flat?*

Then I want you to really think: *How can I be unapologetically ambitious? How can I put myself out there in a bigger, bolder way?*

YOU NEED TO BECOME UNAPOLOGETICALLY AMBITIOUS

Being unapologetically ambitious means truly owning and understanding the value that you bring to your organization. If you're not already being unapologetically ambitious, it means that there is part of you that doesn't trust.

And it's okay. It's normal when we go for really big things. But you need to start noticing this, because we can spend all day long trying to convince our boss, the leadership team, or the CEO that they should promote us into a higher-level executive position. But if we don't trust in our ability to do that job and to really excel at that job, it's going to be really hard to convince anybody else.

Plus, if you're somebody who knows that you should schedule a meeting with somebody important or have that difficult conversation and you're not doing it, it's because you don't trust yourself.

Now, notice that I didn't say that you trust yourself in that "I'm going to understand all of the details and I'm going to be an incredible CFO, and I know that I'm just going to knock it out of the park because I have so much amazing knowledge" way.

No. This kind of trust means that you know your value and that you trust that you can lead at that higher executive level. It doesn't mean you trust that you have everything you need *right now* to be an exceptional C-suite leader. It means knowing that you are resourceful enough to figure it out and ambitious enough to actually go for it.

You understand why it matters for YOU to be a high-level leader in your organization.

I'm not just talking about being recognized for the work you do or earning more money. Instead, I want to know why it matters to have you in a different title than the one you have today.

It's important because of the impact and influence that you, personally (because you are amazing), could have at a higher executive level.

BE MORE PROACTIVE ABOUT BUILDING TRUST WITH THE LEADERSHIP TEAM

The next thing you're going to do is be very proactive about the relationships you are building at your organization.

There is a process that I teach in my Executive Ahead of Time program called 15-Minute Ally Meetings. They're very simple yet incredibly effective. Here's how they work. You're going to start scheduling 15-Minute Ally Meetings on a regular basis with everyone around you. When you have these meetings, you are going to be talking about how you're ready for growth, and you're going to be sharing your 3× Vision.

This means you're going to be talking about your professional development at times *other* than your performance review time. These are just going to be simple, open, and honest conversations.

THE ORIGIN OF 15-MINUTE ALLY MEETINGS

I created this process in response to the COVID-19 pandemic, because I had so many clients complaining that they no longer had face time with executive leadership.

You know what I mean. Bumping into members of the leadership team in the hallway. Popping into someone's office on the way to lunch.

Once everyone started working virtually, my clients needed a way to connect with leadership. That is why I created the 15-Minute Ally Meeting. It's brilliant for two reasons:

1. Anyone, even busy executives, is willing to meet with you for fifteen minutes.
2. They are so short and concise, they really do replicate the "bumping into someone in the hallway" outcome.

Through the process of conducting 15-Minute Ally Meetings,

you're going to create alliances across your organization. The people who seemingly come out of nowhere and advocate for you and say, "You know what? I have a really amazing opportunity for you."

They not only *say* they have a great opportunity for you, but they actually go to bat for you and make sure that you actually get that opportunity.

You know those people, right? The ones who will actually speak up on your behalf and create opportunities for you. You can go out and create those allies for yourself right now. The process to get there is called 15-Minute Ally Meetings.

TRUST IS BUILT BETWEEN THE MEETINGS

Simon Sinek is a brilliant speaker and the author of *Start with Why*. One of the things he talks about is this idea that trust is built between the meetings.

He describes it as those words you exchange with someone walking into or out of the meeting.

For example, you're standing next to somebody, and you're like, "Hey, how are your kids?" Or, "Oh my gosh. The summer has been brutal, right?" Or perhaps you're talking about the meeting that's coming up. But it's all those side conversations that build trust.

According to Sinek, one of the best ways to think about it is someone's relationship with their partner. They didn't fall in love with them because of the date itself. They fell in love with them because of the connection they had with them. Those little things in between the dates. The little things in between the meetings are what build trust with leadership. What's missing right now? Those little things in between the meetings.

BEING MORE PROACTIVE ABOUT THESE CONVERSATIONS IS A GOOD THING

I had a woman reach out to me very early in March 2020, just as offices were starting to shut down because of the pandemic. She said, "One of the biggest things I miss since we turned virtual is that I used to see my boss in the hallway. I used to just walk past him, and then we would chat for a little bit. Then I would notice that in the meeting, he would actually call on me more often."

So I coached her to actively go out and have those conversations with her boss before the meeting and not rely on the hallway conversation.

Plus, it turned out to actually be a good thing that she couldn't just rely on her old habits of walking past someone at the watercooler any longer.

Why is this such a good thing? Because proactively building

relationships puts her in the driver's seat of her career. She's going out and scheduling those conversations. Ultimately, it builds more trust with leadership.

What I recommend to my clients today is they need to stop relying on bumping into people in the hallway altogether and schedule a 15-Minute Ally Meeting with that person instead.

WHO SHOULD YOU SCHEDULE A 15-MINUTE ALLY MEETING WITH?

Now, you're probably already having one-on-one meetings with your boss on a regular basis, so let's say that trust has already been built with them.

Instead, I want you to schedule meetings with the leaders who you are not already meeting with one-to-one on a regular basis.

PERSON #1

The person you should consider reaching out to first is your boss's boss.

If you feel that this would be going over your boss's head, then be transparent. Let your boss know that you are scheduling this meeting and why—to build a better relationship. That's all. It doesn't have to be anything more.

PERSON #2

You might be apprehensive about this, but the next person that you should be reaching out to is your CEO.

Now, I don't know how large your corporation is. If it's a gigantic corporation and your CEO is extremely far out of reach, don't worry about it. They're probably a little bit too far away. But if they're within arm's reach (like my client who used to actually pass her CEO all the time in the hallway), then you should schedule a 15-Minute Ally Meeting with them starting *yesterday*.

PERSON #3

The third person is whoever you want it to be!

Pick someone. Think of somebody that you used to see on a regular basis that you miss seeing. It could be really anybody.

When we're talking about leveraging our relationships and actually building our career, then I suggest a peer, a member of the leadership team, somebody above you who you're used to seeing on a regular basis but you're just not seeing anymore. Whoever that is.

HOW TO SCHEDULE A 15-MINUTE ALLY MEETING

The benefits of only requesting fifteen minutes of someone's time are:

1. It's really low pressure for the person you're asking.
2. It shows that you respect their time.
3. It shows that this will be a casual conversation and not an energy-draining deep dive into something really big.

When you're reaching out to schedule the meeting, you want to make it clear that you're scheduling a meeting to connect, not to bring them problems to help you solve.

The reason why is because framing it as a problem in need of solving gives them an out. They're going to read that and think, *Oh. Well, that's not really something that I can help her with. I'm just going to ignore this email. It doesn't really seem like it fits me.*

Here's what to say instead: "I want to connect with you because I haven't seen you in three months. I'm asking for a fifteen-minute meeting."

That's it. Super simple.

Show them that you miss seeing them on a regular basis, and you just want to have a quick check-in. You could tell them that you want to see what they're up to, see what their challenges are, and give a quick update on what you're working on. Especially if it's somebody who you used to see physically and you don't anymore. Make sure you tell them that and that you value the time with them.

If you're somebody who hasn't already had that relationship, then just say, "I'm trying to be more proactive about my relationship building along with communicating and connecting with leadership. Can I schedule a fifteen-minute call on your calendar just to do a quick check-in?"

That's it.

You're going to get out there and schedule those meetings right away. Don't hesitate. Plus, it takes a long time to get on their calendar. You want to reach out right now before you second-guess it. Before you're ready. Just schedule the conversation, get on their calendar, and just do it. It's fifteen minutes. It's a simple thing. But it could make such a difference in your career this year. Your boss can't be the only person who supports you. If you're somebody who has a boss who doesn't support them, you really know what I mean. It's important to build that trust with everyone else around you.

Just like Simon Sinek pointed out, trust is built in between the meetings.

Get it scheduled. Do it now. Just rip off the Band-Aid, and I guarantee it is going to help you so much. It's going to help your confidence. It's going to help your career, and it's going to help you get promoted into a senior executive leadership position even faster.

EXACTLY WHAT SHOULD HAPPEN IN A 15-MINUTE ALLY MEETING

Now that you've scheduled those 15-Minute Ally Meetings, the next step is to understand what to actually do in the meeting.

#1: STAY INTERESTED

The most important thing you need to do is to stay interested.

You're going to share what is working. I want you to share a win (something that is going well). For example, I just got assigned to this new high-profile project, and I am excited about the impact potential.

#2: ASK POWERFUL QUESTIONS

Don't be afraid to ask questions. If the leader you are speaking with talks for nearly the entire meeting, that's a good thing. When people talk more, they feel like the meeting went really well.

So let them talk and, when you can, ask powerful questions. You can do this by digging a little bit deeper. What's going on for them? What is their vision? What are their values? What is working for them?

#3: SCHEDULE THE NEXT MEETING

I cannot harp on this enough. Before the end of the meeting, when you're still actually in the meeting, schedule the next one.

You could say something like, "Well, this went really great. You know what I was wondering? Can we do this again next month, just another fifteen-minute meeting? I would love to make this a regular thing."

This is so, so, so important, because once you get out of the meeting, scheduling the next one takes way too long. So don't be afraid to plan what you're going to say ahead of time, and actually ask for the next meeting.

Note: While you're having this 15-Minute Ally Meeting, always remember this isn't the place to discuss all your problems or bring up your professional development. This is just a really quick, simple 15-Minute Ally Meeting. It's a relationship-building meeting.

WHY YOU NEED TO START MAKING ALLIES TODAY

If even 10 percent of the leadership team trusts that you're ready for that next level, that's all you need to start elevating your leadership, having a voice at the table, and being earmarked for exciting new promotions.

So go out and start scheduling your 15-Minute Ally Meetings today.

CHAPTER SUMMARY

- To make it to high-level leadership positions, you need to build trust with the leadership team that you can do the job at a senior executive level.
- Building this kind of trust is so important because you want *other people* to advocate on your behalf.
- You need to be proactive about the relationships you are building at your organization. You can do this via 15-Minute Ally Meetings. When you have these meetings, you are going to be talking about how you're ready for growth, and you're going to be sharing your 3× Vision.
- Start with scheduling 15-Minute Ally Meetings with these three people: your boss's boss, your CEO, a third person of your choosing (this can be anyone!).
- During a 15-Minute Ally Meeting, remember these three things: 1) Stay interested; 2) Ask powerful questions; and 3) Schedule the next meeting.

ACTION STEPS

1. Select three people to schedule a 15-Minute Ally Meeting with. I recommend you choose:
- Your boss's boss.
- Your CEO (or another senior executive leader if your CEO is out of reach).
- Whoever you want it to be! I suggest a peer, a member of the leadership team, or somebody above you who you're used to seeing on a regular basis but you're just not seeing anymore.

2. Schedule your 15-Minute Ally Meeting, and use these simple messages to schedule your meeting:
- If you already have a relationship with this person, you can say, "I want to connect with you because I haven't seen you in three months. I'm asking for a fifteen-minute meeting."
- If you don't already have a relationship with this person, you can say, "I'm trying to be more proactive about my relationship building, along with communicating and connecting with leadership. Can I schedule a fifteen-minute call on your calendar just to do a quick check-in?"

3. Make the most of your time.
- Examples of questions to ask at these meetings include what they're working on, what their goals are, and what their challenges are.

4. Schedule a follow-up conversation.
- Don't worry about what you will discuss at the follow-up meeting. That answer will come later. For now, just get it on the calendar.

Download free resource guides at stacymayer.com/resources.

CHAPTER 7

THE PERFORMANCE REVIEW PROBLEM

For the majority of corporate leaders, performance review time goes something like this:

- They worked super hard all year long and met every single deadline.
- Their team loves them.
- They have produced extraordinary results.

So they walk into their boss's office at review time expecting a promotion…only to leave with a modest pay increase, kudos, and a pat on the back.

If you've experienced this, you're not alone.

The reality is, performance review time is the worst possible time to advocate for a promotion. That's because you need to start advocating for your promotion *long before* you walk into your boss's office to discuss your performance.

Here's an example of what I mean. When I first begin working with a client, it's common for them to reach out to me in tears because they got passed over for a promotion at review time.

One client, a senior director of strategy, complained on our coaching call that she had received "highly effective" on her performance review, and she was upset about it. She even received the highest pay increase she was eligible for, but she was still frustrated.

This didn't sit well with her because she knew she was meant for more. She stopped feeling frustrated and got to work. It became a running joke in our coaching. I would remind her, "Do you want to be rated as highly effective or do you want a promotion?"

She started communicating her strategy instead of the details, she 3×ed her vision, and she built trust with leadership using 15-Minute Ally Meetings. Now she proudly holds the title of vice president.

HOW TO GET A PROMOTION AT PERFORMANCE REVIEW TIME (OR BEFORE)

I want to take a moment and acknowledge that *yes* you *can* land a promotion at performance review time. But wouldn't it feel better to get in the driver's seat of your career? To feel empowered? To know exactly what you need to do to get a promotion again?

Getting in the driver's seat of your career means not waiting until performance review time to speak about your professional development goals or to request feedback on your performance and your ability to get promoted.

But you're probably waiting until performance review time to do these things, just because...well, you have to, right?

Not anymore.

Now for the good news.

When you understand why waiting for performance reviews to advocate for your career is such a bad idea, *you can do something about it.*

IT'S TIME TO START THINKING LIKE AN EXECUTIVE

Regardless of whether or not a performance review is coming

up, you need to start having professional development conversations with your boss—all year long.

Look at it this way. Let's say Christmas is coming up in a month, and you're wondering if Santa Claus is going to bring you gifts. You're not sure if you've been naughty or nice, so you're feeling nervous and unsure of what to expect.

Now, Santa has already decided who's getting gifts and who's not. But you don't know that.

So you spend the entire month of December trying to be as nice as possible to make sure you're going to get a gift. But Santa has already made up his mind.

You wake up on Christmas morning and hope for the best. But as you go to look for your presents…there's nothing there.

The same is true for your performance review.

You're putting that same amount of pressure on somebody else's decisions that were already decided long before the actual performance review date.

So for a few weeks leading up to your performance review, you're thinking, *Oh my gosh, I hope they accept me.* But there's very little that you can do about it at that stage.

Putting your promotion in someone else's hands like that? It's full-on torture. You're walking on pins and needles, wondering if they're going to accept you.

Besides, just like Santa Claus in my example, the leadership team already knows who's getting the gift of a promotion (and who's not) well before your performance review.

You're trying to have an impact on a decision after it's already been decided, and you're stressing yourself out needlessly as a result.

That's why I teach my clients to take their professional development back into their own hands by giving them the tools to get themselves promoted into senior executive leadership.

One of the ways I do this is to teach them how to become the Executive Ahead of Time.

Becoming the Executive Ahead of Time means developing the skills you need to succeed in an executive role before you ever step into one.

It means being a shoo-in for your next promotion, because you know how to do the job already.

It requires you to learn how to advocate for your next

promotion, think, communicate, and lead like a C-suite executive, and be accountable for your own growth and development.

WHAT ACTUALLY MATTERS WHEN IT COMES TO YOUR PERFORMANCE REVIEW

Performance reviews accomplish two things:

1. They give you feedback on your performance.
2. They are an opportunity to recognize your accomplishments with a promotion or higher compensation.

The only thing that matters is the second one.

As I mentioned above, whether or not you are getting a promotion at your next performance review was already decided weeks or even months in advance.

As a result, it's now outside of your control.

It doesn't have much to do with your self-assessment.

It doesn't even matter how your boss feels about you.

It has to do with the allotment in terms of salary for that year (or whether raises are being withheld).

In short, it has to do with lots of things that have very little to do with you.

PROMOTION ENTITLEMENT

Now, you might be thinking to yourself, *But I have put in the hours. I have put in the years at my job, and darn it, I am entitled to a promotion.*

And I agree. You do deserve a promotion. But feeling entitled to a promotion could actually be holding you back from getting the promotion that you so rightfully deserve.

This is a huge blind spot for so many of my clients. They don't even realize that this is the way they're behaving.

BECOMING AWARE OF PROMOTION ENTITLEMENT

Having an awareness that you are feeling or acting entitled to get a promotion could be enough to let go of the frustration that you might be feeling right now because you're not getting promoted.

So you notice it, right? Then the question is, what are you going to do about it? How are you going to actually go after that promotion?

Here's how.

This happened to a client of mine. Neeru had taken a lateral move at a new organization, but she wasn't actually managing people anymore. At her previous organization, she was managing a group of about ten people. So she had a lot of people-leading experience. Unfortunately, she wasn't able to land a people-leading role at her new organization.

When she hired me, she had been at this new organization for three years. In her mind, she thought that it would be a seamless move into a higher-level management position. But her boss kept telling her the famous catch-22, that you can't get promoted into a more senior level management position until you have people-leading experience.

So, of course, the question is how do you get people-leading experience without getting promoted into higher-level management positions?

So, naturally, Neeru felt stuck and frustrated. I noticed that when we first started coaching together, she was really hung up on the fact that she had a people-leading role at her previous organization. That's what she kept saying. "They should understand, because I have all this experience. I do have experience."

That meant, to me, she had the ability to do the job. I had the utmost confidence in her that she could do the job. She had confidence in herself that she could do the job at a higher management level. Her boss, on the other hand, did not have confidence that she could do the job. And she wasn't going to be able to convince her by waving her résumé in her boss's face.

Neeru also couldn't convince her boss to put her up for promotion into a management position because she felt entitled. She thought her previous experience should be enough, but it wasn't. So, through coaching, we broke that down.

I asked her, "Can you see her point of view? She hasn't seen you lead people. She doesn't know you as a people-leader. She has known you for three years, yes, as a manager of projects, as a manager of other people's teams, and as a manager of your peers. But she hasn't seen you lead direct reports."

We had to figure out ways that we could show her manager that she was fully capable. Not only fully capable, but that she was highly qualified and ready to take on that position. That became our work through coaching—how we were going to show that. How we were going to get other executives on her side so that she could seamlessly transition into a leading role. But she was never going to get there if she kept thinking, *Well, they should give it to me based on my résumé.*

You're never going to get to the place that you want to get to if you just continue to feel entitled.

This is the process that I'm talking about. Once you create the awareness around the entitlement, that is when we can get to work. That is when we can actually take action and begin to advance your career to that next level that you deserve. You really do deserve it. I'm not saying that you don't deserve it. I'm just saying that acting entitled creates frustration, which doesn't actually get you to the goal that you want.

Now, here's something else that I want to point out to you. You have probably seen other people at your organization who act entitled and get promoted into senior executive leadership positions. We've all seen it happen. Somebody who is very entitled acts very entitled and then gets rewarded for it, essentially. But what ends up happening at the end of the day is that they may or may not be successful at that job.

IT'S A GOOD THING YOU HAVEN'T BEEN PROMOTED (REALLY)

I conducted a stakeholder interview for the client I mentioned earlier. She was frustrated that she hadn't landed a people-leading role, so I asked her boss about it. It was really interesting, because her boss's answer didn't match up to the reasons my client had been imagining.

Her boss explained to me that the reason why she didn't get the promotion was because the specific peers in her department that she would be responsible for leading had way more tenure than my client did. So her boss worried that she had these two things going against her: she had never been in a people-leading role at their organization, and she hadn't led people at this organization with twenty years of individual contributor experience.

In reality, her boss was actually just looking out for her. She told me, "I would be more than happy to put her up for a promotion in a different department. I would be more than happy to sponsor her in a people-leading role in a different organization."

And now she is happily leading strategy for a team of five engineers.

When you keep focusing on the entitlement, you're really saying to yourself, *I should be able to get this. I should be able to convince them.* But the truth is, you could actually find yourself in the wrong role.

WHAT TO DO DIFFERENTLY IN YOUR PERFORMANCE REVIEW

Now that you understand that promotions are decided ahead of your performance review, and you notice if you are feeling entitled to a promotion or not, what are you going to actually do in your performance review?

UNDERSTAND THAT YOUR PERFORMANCE REVIEW IS A ONE-WAY CONVERSATION

Your promotion has already been decided. So when you're in your performance review, understand that this feedback is to help you get promoted next year. So look at it like that.

Listen to the feedback. It's not the time to negotiate or argue.

(Side note: arguing doesn't mean yelling at your boss. Arguing can also mean not listening or getting frustrated.)

Let's go back to the Santa Claus analogy for a second.

Imagine that you go into the living room and there are no presents, but Santa is sitting on a chair.

You start to argue with him. You say, "I did this, and I did that." And he's listening, but he has a lot more houses to visit this evening. He doesn't have a lot of time for you, and besides, his hands are tied. He doesn't have a present for you. All the presents he has have been allotted for other people. You're fighting for your presents at the wrong time. The same, of course, is true for your promotion.

ASK QUESTIONS INSTEAD

Again, we're listening, not arguing, but we can still ask questions.

Questions like:

"What does this mean?"

Or...

"What would I need to do differently?"

Or...

"It sounds like a lot of things are working, but what is next for me?"

You're not going to state your case as to why you should have been promoted this year instead of next year. You're just going to get super curious and have a very open dialogue with your boss.

OWN YOUR PROFESSIONAL DEVELOPMENT

Now you've heard your performance review. You've listened, you got curious and asked questions, and you've digested the information.

I also want you to schedule a follow-up conversation for two months down the road.

Every two months, you're going to have a conversation with

whoever is in charge of writing your performance review, and you're going to discuss your progress—what's working and what's not working. Essentially, you're going to get ongoing, open feedback from your boss.

This works in two ways:

1. It's a great way to calibrate if you're doing well and provide a clear path as you continue to grow.
2. Your boss will be saying, over and over again and out loud, that you're making progress.

The more your boss gives you specific feedback that you can go out and implement *and* sees that it is working, then it will be much easier to see what you'll be receiving at performance review time.

No more pins and needles. No more wondering if you were "good" enough.

You've been having open and honest discussions with your boss, and now you know exactly what to expect.

This is the *best* kind of performance review. You know what to expect. It's clear. It's just transactional.

HOW TO HAVE FOLLOW-UP CONVERSATIONS

Instead of sitting down and waiting for your boss to tell you how you're doing, always start the conversation with what you have been trying.

So, for example, instead of saying, "Hey, I've delegated more to my team. Do you think it's working?" say, "I received this feedback from you, so I tried this, this, and this. I think it's working, but I still have some room for growth here and here. What are your thoughts about this so far?"

Framing it this way is easier for your boss, and it shows that you are being proactive.

Plus, it's showing that you are capable of executive leadership, because that's how executives communicate. They explain what they're working on and ask for very specific, tailored advice.

That's what you're going to do.

You're going to own the fact that waiting until performance review time and putting all your eggs in one basket is an absurdity. You're going to focus on the ways that you can get some wins and share them throughout the year.

You're going to think beyond performance review time, too. If your company has a hard-and-fast rule that title changes only happen at a certain time of year, ask yourself if that's actually true. Have you noticed other people getting promoted despite that rule?

Advocate for your promotion year-round instead of wondering why your coworker is getting promoted and you aren't. You'll be the one attracting opportunities. You'll feel confident. Your ideas will actually matter. And you will be excited about your job again.

CHAPTER SUMMARY

- Performance review time is the worst possible time to advocate for a promotion. Why? Because it was already decided who was getting a promotion weeks or months before your performance review meeting.
- Regardless of whether or not a performance review is coming up, you need to be having professional development conversations with your boss—*all year long*.
- Feeling entitled to a promotion could actually be holding you back from getting the promotion that you so rightfully deserve because it creates frustration, which doesn't actually get you to the goal that you want.
- What to do differently in your actual performance review: 1) Understand that your performance review is a one-way conversation; 2) Ask questions; and 3) Own your professional development.
- Begin advocating for your career *now*, not before your

next performance review. Every two months, have a conversation with your boss and discuss your progress (what's working and what's not working).

CHAPTER 8

HOW TO ADVOCATE FOR YOUR PROMOTION

In this chapter, I'm going to show you how to start speaking up, raising your hand, and asking for what you want. But as I'm sure you know, that can be easier said than done.

That's why it's important to think about advocating for a promotion as building trust with leadership by letting them know that you are ready to lead at a higher executive level. This means doing things like speaking up in meetings, connecting your ideas back to your company's objectives, raising your hand for opportunities that will give you more exposure to leadership, demonstrating that you are ready for growth, AND simply letting leadership know about your career ambitions.

How you will do that is by becoming your own best sponsor.

A sponsor is the person who advocates on your behalf. They speak up and share about all the awesome things you are doing, and they want the world to know about them. Essentially your sponsor is someone who wants to shout your good tidings from the rooftop.

You might already do that for someone on your team, right? Somebody that you love speaking about and sharing their praises. You love punting to them at meetings because they're just so great, and everything they say is perfect. Now, I want you to start doing that for yourself.

You are your own best advocate for your career advancement. If you start to think of yourself as your own sponsor, you'll quickly discover that you need to develop skills that will help you speak up about your abilities, offer solutions to problems, share with your boss, take control of your own professional development goals, and stop waiting to be asked.

So I want you to start really thinking about this. Use this as a mantra over the next few weeks. Say to yourself, "I am my own best sponsor," and see if that triggers you into action.

THE PROMOTION PITCH

In this chapter, I am going to show you how to advocate

for your promotion in everyday conversation. But there are some times when you need to do a more formal promotion pitch.

A graduate from my Executive Ahead of Time group coaching intensive received a skip-level promotion shortly after the program was finished. How did she do it? She pitched herself from her 3× Vision.

She was a senior manager of business development at a fast-growing technology company in Silicon Valley. Her organization has a formal promotion process where she is required to present a slide deck to the executive team. At this presentation, I encouraged her to speak to her 3× Vision, which was to become a vice president of business development someday.

The presentation went great, and she was fairly confident that she would at least receive a promotion to a director-level role. So when her boss came back with the announcement that she would receive a senior director position instead, she was almost in disbelief. So much so that when she shared the news with me, she shrugged it off as if there must have been a lot of promotions offered at the same time.

Nope. When the promotions were officially announced, she quickly realized that only three other colleagues were promoted that cycle, and she was certainly the only skip level.

That is the power of advocating for your promotion the right way.

WHY ADVOCATING FOR YOUR CAREER IS NONNEGOTIABLE

Up until this point in your career, your work has spoken for itself. For example, if you are in an individual contributor or project management role, that means that success is determined by hitting all your deadlines.

But when it comes to higher-level leadership positions, your work can't do the talking anymore. You have to be willing to talk *about* your work.

Once you get into higher-level senior leadership roles, once you get into a director level, once you start managing other managers, it's critical that you're able to articulate your abilities. Not only that, but you need to be having regular conversations about your best fit, what you do well, what you want to be inspired by, what's inspiring you, offering solutions to much bigger problems, and, most importantly, not waiting to be asked for what you need. As soon as you get into management, it is so important that you start developing the skill.

You don't want to wait until you get into that higher-level role to develop it either. I want you to be thinking, *I need to be as proactive about my career development as I am about my team hitting their deadlines.*

That's why I'm offering you these skills in this chapter. So that, even if you are in the early stages of management, you can start shifting this behavior. This is going to be critical to your ability to perform at those higher levels.

If you're already at the higher levels, but you're noticing that you're not really getting the projects that you want, you're not yet making the impact that you want to be making at your organization. It's because you're not able to speak up in a way that actually enlists trust with the organization.

They need to be able to trust that you can lead the organization at that higher level. One of the ways that they can start trusting you is if you're taking your own professional development seriously, if you can lead your own career development path, and if you can lead other people at that higher level.

It's that simple. You just have to speak up.

You need to start by telling your boss what you want out of your career. But the question is…why *aren't* you already doing it?

THE THREE REASONS YOU'RE NOT ALREADY TELLING YOUR BOSS ABOUT YOUR CAREER VISION

#1: YOU DON'T REALIZE HOW IMPORTANT IT IS

You don't know what you don't know, right? Maybe you just never really thought about it, or you didn't know that it was important. Or maybe you're the type of person who knows that it's important but doesn't actually know the skillset to do it stealthily.

#2: YOU DON'T KNOW HOW TO SPEAK UP

How can you advocate for a promotion during a crisis, lay-offs, or a massive change in your organization? How do you speak up when your manager doesn't want to hear about your own professional development?

It may seem impossible at times, but there is always a way to advocate for your career so that other people can hear you *and* advocate on your behalf.

#3: YOU'VE GOTTEN HURT IN THE PAST

This is a big one. Let's say you had some bad experiences with your boss or bad experiences speaking up, and part of the reason why it felt so bad was because it felt ego-driven. Or perhaps your attempts just fell flat. So you think to yourself, *I'm never going to do that again.*

If you can relate to any of the above, it's okay. It happens to the best of us.

ADVOCATING FOR YOUR CAREER *ISN'T* SELFISH

In terms of being your own sponsor, or having your own back, that trust that you can do the work, that trust that you understand the vision for your organization, that knowledge that you really care about the impact that you're going to make...when I put it that way, does it sound ego-driven? No.

If you're reading this book, I know you're not ego-driven. If you were, you wouldn't be looking for what I'm offering. Because you know that what I'm offering is true and authentic, and everything that is going to come out of your mouth when you're advocating for your career is going to come from a pure place of genuinely wanting to serve the organization at a higher level.

If you are somebody who hates using "I" language, or hates talking about what you've done, I want you to know that I get it. But let me tell you, by not doing it, you are not serving your organization to your full potential. So if you can't do it for yourself and for what it will actually give you, and how it will benefit you in your career, then do it for other people. Do it for your organization.

Having you in a higher-level leadership position is going to benefit them to no end. Having other leaders in your organization look up to you, having them use you as a role model, having them want to work on your team because you are the best boss is going to benefit other people.

It's not pushy to let other people know what your ideas are, and what you are seeing in the organization. It is not pushy to speak up when you see that there's a problem. It is not pushy to notice something that you do really well and want to do more of that. These are not pushy things.

THE PROCESS TO BECOME YOUR OWN BEST SPONSOR

I was a professional actress for many, many years. One year I took my one-woman show to the Edinburgh Fringe Festival in Scotland. A friend of mine attended, and he loved my show. He was an amazing sponsor for me. He would walk around all day telling people how amazing I was.

I remember thinking, *I'm glad I have him, because I couldn't do any of this.*

Fast-forward to today, and I now understand how absolutely absurd this idea was.

Advocating for your promotion can just be part of your everyday conversation. Here's what I mean. I am not telling you that I want you to go around all day talking about how amazing you are. No. Let other people do that.

What I am telling you to do is way, way simpler than that. Here is the way that you can actually advocate for your promotion this week.

STEP #1: FIND SOMETHING YOU ENJOY

Before you schedule the meeting, think about a responsibility you have been given that you actually enjoy. Something that is going well that you didn't get to do before. Something that's fun for you but also feels like it's challenging you.

STEP #2: SCHEDULE A MEETING WITH YOUR BOSS

If you don't already have regular one-on-one meetings with your boss, get on your boss's calendar now.

I'm assuming that most of your one-on-ones are usually just task updates. So just go through all of the different things that you're working on (and if you're not discussing tasks with your boss, but having bigger-picture conversations, then congrats! That's the goal). But going over your scorecard isn't the goal for this meeting. I want you to tell your boss that you want to talk about bigger projects. So don't just ask to tack on a few minutes to the end of your last meeting. Ask for a separate meeting.

STEP #3: BRING IT BACK TO THE THINGS YOU ENJOY

When you get in, I want you to tell your boss about those things that you learned in Step #1—the things you're actually enjoying doing, those projects that you're taking on now that are really enjoyable.

WHY YOU NEED TO "BRAG" ABOUT YOUR ACCOMPLISHMENTS

Have you ever heard of the humble brag? If this phrase is in your vocabulary right now, it's got to go if you want to become a senior executive leader.

I've seen this phrase used a lot by corporate managers who want to feel more comfortable bragging about their accomplishments by showing that they're not actually bragging—they're just *humbly* bragging.

The problem with framing it like this is that it implies that bragging about the amazing things you've accomplished is bad and that you have to do it humbly in order to do it at all. I want you to completely banish this notion from your mind.

As a senior executive leader, you need to be able to speak to your accomplishments. In fact, it's your job. It's your job to build trust with the board, with the executive team, and with your CEO. Here's why. As we've been discussing throughout this chapter, *your boss cannot be the only person at your organization who knows about all the incredible things you've done.* Think of how much easier it would be for your boss to put you up for a promotion if the entire leadership team had already heard about your accomplishments.

So instead of thinking about it as a "humble brag," think about it as showing up as the Executive Ahead of Time.

Showing up like an executive leader means you're constantly sharing your core values, your ideas, your accomplishments, and the things you're proud of. This is bragging in a way that actually builds trust with the executive team that you are, in fact, ready to lead at a higher executive level.

You're going to have to get over your fear of bragging.

THE CASE FOR "BRAGGING"

I have a personal story about the fear of bragging.

One day, my husband pointed out that our daughter brags a lot. She was five years old at the time. She was always super proud of her accomplishments, and she wanted to tell everyone about them.

My husband shared with me that as a child, he was told that smart people don't brag. He was above average in his class, and he was very quiet about it. He didn't brag about it. He was actually told by his parents that it's not something that we brag about. "Don't talk about our accomplishments. It's just not something that we do."

This made so much sense to me. I thought, *No wonder it's so difficult for people to speak up for themselves! Because they're being told in so many different ways that it's not okay to brag.*

I did some research and tried to see if there's actually any good messaging out in the world that tells us, as human beings, that it is a good thing to brag.

It's really, really difficult to come across. Instead, we're told things like smart people don't brag or "don't show off." Or that braggers are self-absorbed and only care about themselves.

We have evidence of this. We have evidence of people around us, constantly, who annoy us all the time because all they do is brag. So it's no wonder that people have such difficulty putting themselves and their accomplishments out there.

I get it. You don't want to be seen as the coworker who brags about themself all the time. You don't want to be the self-absorbed person who just seems like they're only out for themself to get that promotion—sort of like the issue with my daughter, who is putting my son down by bragging about her accomplishments. But that is very different from her just being genuinely enthusiastic and excited about her accomplishments.

DEBUNKING THE "BRAGGING" MYTH

The first way that I want to debunk this myth for you is to make sure you understand that when you transition from being seen as a subject matter expert into executive leadership, your job responsibility changes.

Here is what I mean by that. As you continue to move up the ladder, it is an expectation that you become a salesperson for *yourself*. Not necessarily a salesperson for the organization, but a salesperson for your own leadership. That is how people get ahead in their careers at the senior executive level.

It doesn't have to be sleazy. It doesn't have to be narcissistic. It doesn't have to be self-absorbed. Here's the kicker: while modesty is the best course of action in most times of our lives, in most ways, if you're too modest and you're expecting to get promoted into senior executive positions, the result will just be that you won't get promoted.

Let's think about it from a sales perspective. If you're a salesperson and you don't talk about your product, you don't actually want to share about all the features and the accomplishments of your product and what it can do and the value that it can bring to the consumer, you're not going to have any sales. People are simply not going to buy your product.

Now, if you've ever met a really skillful salesperson—not the sleazy, bragging type of salesperson, but a really skillful salesperson—it feels good to be sold to by them. You know why it feels good to be sold to in that way? Because you *trust* them. You're putting your money down, and whatever product you're buying, you trust that it's going to deliver.

The same is true for you. Bragging in a good way instills trust in leadership that you can lead at that senior executive level.

WHEN TO BRAG (AND WHEN NOT TO)

Now, I want to give you a funny example of how bragging can go off the rails.

I found this example online from an article in *Psychology Today* about why not to brag. Now, imagine you won a gold medal. That's great! You have every right to be very proud of this accomplishment. And it's okay to write about this accomplishment in your bio, to share it on social media, things like that. But it's *not* okay to wear the gold medal around your neck when you go to the grocery store. That is bragging in the worst sense of the word.

The same thing goes for sharing your accomplishments at work. There is a time and a place and a way that is appropriate (and *NOT* so appropriate).

You've probably experienced the inappropriateness, too.

For example, let's say you're at a networking event. You've got your elevator pitch ready, and someone you just met asks you, "So, what do you do?"

You dive into your elevator pitch. You say, "'I graduated from here, I work at this organization, we're the top-ranked company in XYZ...' and on and on.

This feels very braggy, right? Because the other person is looking at you like a deer in headlights, thinking, *I can't wait to get out of this conversation as fast as possible.*

And it doesn't feel good because you notice it. You think, *Wow, that backfired. I'm never going to do that again.*

No! You just need to do it better. And the way that we get better at communicating is by practicing.

HOW TO PRACTICE BRAGGING THE *RIGHT* WAY

As we've laid out, there is a right time to brag and a wrong one. In this section, I'll be showing you a case study from one of my clients that will help you determine how and when you should brag.

In Chapter 3, I shared about Laura, who is the vice president of human resources at her organization and reports directly to the CEO. Laura is really great at her job. But the problem is she's extremely humble and doesn't toot her own horn. At the same time, she was tired of getting walked over, and she wanted a voice at the table. That's why she hired me.

Now, I do stakeholder interviews for every one of my clients. One day, I was interviewing Laura's boss, the CEO. Her boss really loves her. She thought Laura was really great. But then she said, "I would like to see more of her human resources expertise. If she is going to operate at the CHRO level, she's going to need to demonstrate more of an expertise in human resources."

Laura and I had a meeting, and when I told her what her CEO said, she was confused. She said, "I know a lot about HR. I'm an expert. I have a very strong background. I have a large network. I make conclusions, not based on hunches, but on real evidence."

I probed a little bit deeper, and I asked, "Do you ever share this with your boss?"

Laura explained that she shared her results, but not her work. So I coached her to actually start to show her work.

Here's what she had to do.

She had to go back to her boss, and over time, start sliding her work into their conversations together. Not all at once. But over several different conversations. She talked about the HR networks that she belonged to. She shared with her boss how she came up with some of these conclusions, where she did her research, etc., so that her boss could see her as the human resources expert.

What she was really doing as she had these conversations was building trust. And it worked. Once she started sharing this information, her boss quickly started seeing her as the expert she already was.

So Laura became more confident. Her CEO started to call on her more in the leadership meetings. My client realized other areas where she wasn't speaking up. So she started to speak up there, too. Then eventually she started to do a lot of work on her own. Really taking big initiatives, not waiting to be told what to do. Essentially, she started operating at that CHRO level *ahead of time.*

This is the power of bragging about your accomplishments the right way.

THREE SALES SECRETS YOU CAN USE TO SELL *YOURSELF*

I've talked about how sales and marketing become part of your job description as you advance into senior executive leadership positions. Now I want to give you just three tips I have learned through teaching my clients how to be better advocates for themselves.

#1: BE DIRECT

Being direct can be broken into two parts:

The first thing that I want you to do is just share that you are interested in a senior executive position someday with your boss. It's not an ultimatum. It's simply asking your boss, "What would you need to see me demonstrate if you were to sponsor me for a senior executive position?" Don't beat around the bush. Don't be shady. Just be super, super direct.

The second thing I want you to be direct about is what you're *seeing.* So if you see something, say something. Have you ever been in a meeting and seen a problem flashing like a red light at you? And you thought to yourself, *Oh my gosh. This is such a huge problem, and I know a solution. I know a way to solve this problem.*

So being direct in this case means you're going to raise your hand. You're going to offer solutions to problems. You're going to add ideas. You're going to ask questions. You're going to be a part of the conversation. This is showing your knowledge. It's showing your ideas. It's sharing them in a way that's not saying you have to choose my idea. It's saying I have ideas and I'm not afraid to speak up. This is a very important quality that all C-suite executives must possess. So if you start doing that at whatever level you're at now, you'll start to build that trust that you can lead at that higher executive level.

#2: ADD VALUE

I touched on adding value in the last point, which is that you're actually offering solutions and ideas. But you might be thinking, *I don't know what to say*, and to that, I always say, "But what do you know?"

Figure that out before you go into any meeting with the executive team, or any meeting with your boss, or any meeting with a member of the leadership team. I want you to know the number one thing you want to get out of this conversation. If that thing is to show them your work, your passion, or your desire for something, then make sure that those are the areas you start speaking up about.

#3: OWN IT

It's time to go out there and own it. You're going to own your confidence and the fact that it matters to have you in a senior executive leadership position.

I get it. It's scary to be direct, to speak up, and add value. When I was selling myself and my program to my students, I used to feel very scared to own my value during those sales conversations. Then I realized it was a necessary part of the deal. The same goes for senior executive leadership. It is part of the deal.

BONUS: SHARE STORIES

Earlier I talked about listing your bio to someone at a networking event, and the other person looking like a deer in headlights as a result. Well, the reason why they look like that is because you're literally just listing off your bio, the bullet points of your career. But no. I want you to share a *story*. I want you to share a time that something happened.

Back to my client Laura.

When Laura slips in examples of her work during conversations with her boss, she isn't just telling her, "I belong to three HR networking groups, I graduated from X college," etc.

Instead, she's going to say, "In my HR networking group last week, we were actually talking about retention. One of the things that I brought up was an idea that I've been sharing with you, X, Y, Z."

Do you see what I mean? It's a story. It's not bragging. You're just sharing what you're proud of.

BRAGGING IS PART OF YOUR JOB DESCRIPTION

The reality is, bragging about your accomplishments is part of your job description at the senior executive level. The only way you're going to get to that level is to share about your accomplishments. So you need to get comfortable with it now.

So if you're somebody who grew up thinking that "smart people don't brag" or that you're showing off if you toot your own horn, that's fine. But just know when you are at work, it's part of your job to show your work, to share your accomplishments, and to put yourself out there in a way that adds value to your boss, to your organization, and to the leadership team, so that they can get you promoted.

So put yourself out there. Be bold, and be strong.

CHAPTER SUMMARY

- A sponsor is a person who advocates on your behalf. They speak up and want the world to know about all the awesome things you are doing.
- *You* are your own best advocate for your career advancement. If you start to think of yourself as your own

sponsor, you'll quickly discover that you need to develop skills that will help you speak up about your abilities, offer solutions to problems, share with your boss, take control of your own professional development goals, and stop waiting to be asked.

- The process to becoming your own best sponsor is: 1) Think of a responsibility that you have been given that you enjoy; 2) Schedule a meeting with your boss; and 3) Bring it back to the responsibility that you enjoy.

- As a senior executive leader, being able to speak to your accomplishments is your *job*. Why? You need to be able to build trust with the board, with the executive team, and with your CEO.

- Sales and marketing become part of your job description as you advance into senior executive leadership positions. Here are the three sales techniques you can use to sell yourself: 1) Be direct and raise your hand for opportunities; 2) Add value and show your work; and 3) Own that you belong in a senior executive leadership position.

CHAPTER 9

HOLDING YOURSELF ACCOUNTABLE

In this chapter, I'm going to show you how to hold yourself accountable so that you can actually land that next promotion.

Now, if you've been trying to receive a promotion in the past and you've been working really hard to get there, I want you to know two remaining reasons why you haven't been successful.

One is because you didn't have an actual plan to get a promotion.

Two, if you did have a plan, you didn't stick to it. You didn't commit to it over the long haul.

I'm going to show you how to not only create a plan, but how you can hold yourself accountable along the way.

As you have been reading, you've probably gotten really excited about what's possible. You've probably implemented a strategy or two and seen some wins.

Maybe you have a plan to get out of the weeds, or you're finally speaking more strategically to your boss. You are feeling more confident by understanding and making decisions from the big vision that you have. You know what it means to actually build trust with leadership using 15-Minute Ally Meetings.

Now you're going to put all of that stuff on paper, and you're going to start to notice one really big thing.

You're going to notice if you really *do* want that promotion. Because once it's on paper, it's going to get real. It's going to feel like it might actually happen. That might bring up some things, some uncertainty inside you as to if you're really ready for this.

I want to say that you *are*. I'm going to show you exactly how you can keep that core vision at the forefront.

Because getting promoted is not always about the title, and sometimes it's not even about the pay compensation.

The reason that you really want the recognition that you deserve is because you want your work to actually matter. The higher up you go and the closer you get to a senior executive leadership position, the more you actually see the fruits of your labor.

It's incredible. You already work long hours. You really care about your job. But now, you get to see it actually manifest and show itself in the organization's bottom line. *That is the best thing ever.*

WHY YOU ARE UNABLE TO MAKE PROGRESS

If you feel like your desire for getting a promotion has been there for a long time but you just aren't making forward progress, I want you to know that this is super common. It's why I feel confident that there are easily 1,000 powerhouse corporate women out there ready, qualified, and able to be promoted, and they just aren't getting there.

Why are otherwise high achievers unable to get the promotion and recognition they deserve?

While each person has a unique situation or circumstance, really it keeps coming down to the same two problems. Let me know if you can relate.

1. You are stuck in your immediate situation.

2. You are stuck in indecision.

It's one of those two things. Once you get past whichever is holding you back, that's when the solution presents itself. That's when you know what to do next. That's when you create your Promotion Blueprint and move forward.

WHAT TO DO IF YOU FEEL STUCK IN YOUR IMMEDIATE SITUATION

Let's start with feeling stuck in your immediate situation. What are all the excuses you are telling yourself? I know they don't *feel* like excuses to you. They feel very real.

Here are a few excuses I hear almost daily from potential clients.

- I work for a small company, so there is no clear promotion path.
- My boss doesn't seem to care about my professional development OR worse, she is actively blocking me from getting promoted.
- I have to stay in my particular role for at least two years.
- I am tied to this department because of my expertise or experience.
- Leadership promotions are based on tenure.

Notice I said potential clients because my actual clients are the ones who are willing to let me poke holes in their excuses, and to challenge them. *Some* of them do end up being true. But it's so important to have that willingness to challenge them first.

So ask yourself, *Am I 100 percent certain that this is true?* If there is any doubt whatsoever, that is just something to note.

For instance, I have a client whose boss is blocking her from getting a promotion. That was the initial situation she shared with me. So I coached her to have a conversation with her boss about it.

She listened and did what I said. Turns out she had never actually *asked* her boss why she wouldn't support her to move up into the next level of management. When she asked in this way, her boss told her *why*. So now we have information.

It wasn't that her boss was mean or that she was out to get her. It turns out that her boss wasn't even trying to block her.

Once you can get out of feeling frustrated and stuck in your immediate circumstance—even if it does turn out to be true—then you can create a path to move forward.

WHAT TO DO IF YOU FEEL STUCK IN INDECISION

The second reason why you are stuck and unable to create

your Promotion Blueprint is because you are stuck in indecision. You will know this if:

- You have been talking about "doing something about it" for a while now (six months or more).
- You complain to your spouse regularly about your job but don't actually take steps to improve it.
- You live for the weekends. You can't wait to get home from work. You never want to think about it once you walk out the door.
- You tell yourself that you'll do something about it at the next performance review.
- The most common excuse you give yourself is, "I just need to make a decision."

If this is you, do me a favor and decide with me today. Just make the decision to move forward, even if it's something small. Say, "Okay, Stacy. You got me. I need to do something different."

THE ACCOUNTABILITY PROCESS

Your Promotion Blueprint answers these five questions:

1. What is the long-term vision for my career?
2. What are my top five core values?
3. How am I going to measure my success along the way?

4. What are the steps that I'm going to have to take to get there over the next six months?

5. What are the obstacles that I need to look out for (or what are the obstacles that I'm currently facing)?

I'm going to break that all down for you in this chapter. But I just want you to know that you are not only fully capable of getting a promotion and succeeding at that senior executive level, but now you have a plan to actually get there.

Now, I'll break these down a bit.

IDENTIFYING THE LONG-TERM VISION FOR YOUR CAREER

First, you need to actually know what you want. This is your 3× Vision that we spoke about in Chapter 4, and it's the part where most people get stuck and don't even start. Like I said before, you are experiencing indecision. Now I'm going to invite you to just decide. That's it. It's super simple.

Start with a title. I want to be vice president. I want to be a CFO. I want to be the head of diversity and inclusion. Dream big. It should make you giggle a little because it probably feels ridiculous. That's a good thing.

Once I was speaking to a woman who had recently taken a demotion. She went from managing a team to managing a project all because she moved away from the headquarters. Two years prior, this felt like the right thing to do. But lately, it's been weighing on her. She is now stuck in her immediate circumstance. She can't get over the fact that there are no remote management positions where she is living right now. But I DID get her to admit that she wants to be CFO someday.

And yes, she laughed hard! She even said, "Who am I to be CFO?" But I reminded her, "Who are you *not* to be?"

Now she had something to work with. It immediately jolted her out of the present situation, and now she knew where her work was. If she wants to be CFO someday, she had better stop wallowing in the fact that there are no opportunities where she is currently and get out there and MAKE a new opportunity for herself, even if it's someplace else.

So ask yourself, *What do I want?* Just decide. Then you can start creating a Promotion Blueprint to get there.

IDENTIFYING YOUR CORE VALUES

Return to your notes from Chapter 5 when you identified your unique leadership style. In that chapter, you identified a peak leadership experience. Now we are going to elaborate on that experience and turn it into your core values.

Identify what really stands out to you from that experience.

What were some of the values that you were cultivating at the time? Why did it feel good to you? Write down some of those adjectives for yourself.

Now for part two. I want you to think of a time when things did not go so well in your leadership career. When your career was just really, really challenging, and you could not get ahead. You were very frustrated, and you kept hitting roadblocks.

Identify exactly what was happening at the time. What were some of the core values that were not being met at that time? What were some of the frustrating moments? How does that shed light on what your core values might be? Generally, if you're frustrated, it's because one of your core values is not being met.

Now for part three, you're going to think about your code of conduct and your moral ethics. This is an idea that has been with you since you were a child. Do you believe in hard work, that everything happens for a reason, or do you believe in equality (whatever that is for you)?

So go through each one of these steps: one, two, and three, and really look at what is coming up. Then decide on what your core values actually are. List five words that really stand out to you.

Is it responsibility, trustworthiness, patience, hard work,

authenticity, compassion, meaningful work, recognition, responsibility, or balance? Try to narrow it down to five core values. You could have more than one on a line. Totally fine. That's going to give you your top five values.

Now, I want to give you one word of caution, because this happens all of the time for my clients. You're going to look at this list and you're going to write down the things that you aspire to be. Like, I want to believe in XYZ, but it didn't appear when you were doing the exercises. If it didn't come up when you were sharing your stories, leave it off your list (for now).

The reason why I say that is because unless it really inherently is your gut instinct, it's not going to be as much of a motivator as you continue to rise in your career. Make sure that you have those core values that feel really true to you.

THE VALUE OF GROWTH

I want you to consider adding growth to your list of core values.

You might have listed other subtle things like learning or achievement—things that are similar to growth. But I would like to encourage you to actually put growth into your core values.

Now, you might say, "Well, it's not one of my top five core values."

But in reality, it is.

Because you're reading this book, it means that you want to do something different. It means you want to think outside of the box, and you want to challenge yourself and grow.

The reason why it's so important to have this listed as one of your top five core values is because when we think of growth as an inevitability, as something that we're actually striving toward, when we do fail or when we do come across challenges, we realize that it's all part of our growth.

It's also a reminder that change is inevitable. As part of growth, failure is also inevitable. We're going to have ups, and we're going to have downs. If we plan for that, it makes the downs so much easier to handle.

MEASURING YOUR SUCCESS ALONG THE WAY

Now we are going to put a time frame on your plan. Over the next six months, what outcomes do you realistically hope to achieve that will put you closer to your 3x Vision?

Really think about this. How will you know if you're moving closer toward your goal?

Here are some examples:

- Team members are self-organized and thinking long term.
- My boss has acknowledged that I am improving.
- Operating at a higher strategic level—less reactive.
- Communicating ideas and vision to upper management and to your team.
- Regular conversations with external leaders in a variety of areas.
- Inclusion in management team meetings.
- Get promoted or am in direct line for a promotion.

These are just a few examples, but based on your particular vision and what you feel like your personal challenges are, you're going to start with that. I'd like you to have anywhere between three and five measurements.

THE ACTION STEPS THAT IT WILL TAKE TO GET THERE

Then we're going to think about what you will actually need to DO to accomplish each one of these outcomes.

Get specific. Look at each of your measurements and ask what actions you will need to take to get closer to that outcome.

Here are some examples:

- Before every meeting with my team, remind myself to speak to the vision and not the details.
- Schedule regular 15-Minute Ally Meetings with members of the executive team.
- Block out time in my calendar to strategize.
- Communicate less with my boss about my scorecard and focus more on how my work ties into the long-term vision for my team.
- Research and connect with key industry experts outside of my organization.
- Add value in everyday conversations to set myself up to be included in larger team meetings.
- Request monthly professional development conversations with my boss.

Once these main actions are identified, check back in monthly to make sure you are on track.

UNDERSTAND YOUR OBSTACLES

Next, list out any obstacles that are currently standing in your way.

Now you have completed your five-step Promotion Blueprint.

WHY YOU NEED TO BE CONSISTENT

Congratulations! Most corporate leaders don't even have a plan. They're not sure where they're going, and they certainly don't know how they're going to get there. They just wing it based on however they're feeling, or if they're getting the recognition that they deserve.

But so many people, when asked, aren't exactly sure how to articulate what their actual career goals are aside from their daily performance. So make sure you understand that:

"Success doesn't come from what you do occasionally, it comes from what you do consistently."

—MARIE FORLEO, AUTHOR OF *EVERYTHING IS FIGUREOUTABLE*

I love this quote because it reminds you that success is really about what you do every single day.

Your Promotion Blueprint is not a regular goal-setting document. It is an accountability document. That's because you're simply looking at it and asking yourself, *Can I measure it? Am I moving toward my goals? Am I actually doing what I said I was going to do?*

Keep it simple and easy to understand. It will most likely fit on one page. That way, it's easy to review it on a regular basis (fifteen minutes per month) and take the consistent action you need to get to that next level of leadership (and the next promotion after that, and the next promotion after that).

ONCE YOU IMPLEMENT THESE TEACHINGS, YOU'LL BE IN A LEAGUE OF YOUR OWN

Eighty percent of corporate managers say that they are too busy doing their job to focus on professional development. This is 100 percent the case for all of the clients that come to me.

It's not that they can't get that promotion necessarily. It's that they don't know what it's going to take to actually get to that next level of leadership. They don't know how to measure recognition. They don't know how to hold themselves accountable. They don't know what it means to advocate for themselves, to build trust, to become the Executive Ahead of Time.

Now, you'll be one of the few corporate managers who knows exactly what to say when a member of the leadership team asks you where you want to go in your career.

Once I was speaking to a CIO, and she told me that one of the secrets to her success is that she knew she wanted to be a CIO really early on. She talked about it to everybody who would listen. So make sure you're very clear on where you're headed and why you want to get there.

And schedule it. Pick a day each month to review your Promotion Blueprint. I personally keep a copy in Google Docs so I can make changes. I may review it and ask myself, *Is this still true?* and I change the measurements and methods accordingly.

A lot of times, the obstacles will stay the same or sometimes not. Sometimes they go away. But the vision and the values always stay the same. That's why it takes only fifteen minutes. It's super easy, but it keeps you on track, and it keeps you holding yourself accountable.

Here are some other ways that you can use this document.

When you feel stuck and aren't sure what to do, I want you to ask yourself, *What would I do if I was a CFO? What would I do if I was a CTO? What would I do if I was the CHRO? What would I do if I was the senior vice president?*

Just ask yourself those questions, and it will give you an insight into what it is that you should be doing or what you're holding onto.

I had a client who was actually applying for a job, and she was just asking me all these questions as if we had never created her blueprint. She was very confused if she should take this job. She wasn't applying for it; she was offered the position.

So I said, "Well, let's pull up your Promotion Blueprint."

As soon as we did, it became very clear this was not the job for her. So have your blueprint in front of you when you need to make a decision.

Now I want you to take action. Remember how I said you're going to schedule fifteen minutes a month? That's all you have to do. Go to your calendar, open it up, and put that fifteen-minute reminder in every single month. Let's say the fifth of the month, and remind yourself to review your Promotion Blueprint and hold yourself accountable for reaching your career goals.

CHAPTER SUMMARY

- If you've been struggling to receive a promotion, there are one of two reasons why you haven't been successful until now: 1) You didn't have an actual plan to get a promotion; and 2) If you *did* have a plan, you didn't stick to it. In order to not make these mistakes again, you need to hold yourself accountable.
- Otherwise successful corporate managers aren't able to get the promotion and recognition they deserve due to one of these two problems: 1) You are stuck in your immediate situation; or 2) You are stuck in indecision.
- When you think of growth as a core value, you realize that failure is part of that growth. When you plan for

failure, it makes the inevitable ups and downs so much easier to handle.

- You can begin to move forward by creating a Promotion Blueprint. The five main elements that your Promotion Blueprint must include are: 1) The outcome you want; 2) Identifying your core values; 3) Understanding how to measure your success; 4) The steps you will take to reach your goals; and 5) The obstacles that stand in your way.
- Once you've created your Promotion Blueprint, schedule fifteen minutes per month with yourself to review it.

ACTION STEPS

Understanding that a promotion is not a reward for your hard work means that you are deliberately managing your career.

1. Using the strategies outlined in this chapter or by downloading my worksheet at stacymayer.com/resources, create your own Promotion Blueprint document.
2. Your Promotion Blueprint should include your:
   A. 3× Vision
   B. Core values
   C. Measurements of success
   D. Actions you will take to get there
   E. Any anticipated obstacles along the way
3. Schedule time in your calendar monthly to review and make adjustments.

- As you review it, ask yourself, *Am I moving toward my goals? Am I actually doing what I said I was going to do?*
- When you feel stuck and aren't sure what to do, ask yourself, *What would I do if I was already a (insert your 3× Vision)?*

CHAPTER 10

HOW YOU'LL KNOW IF IT'S WORKING

This chapter might contain the most important lesson in the entire book. That's because if you're trying to change or fix the wrong problem, then you're going to continuously be heading in the wrong direction.

Understanding how to properly evaluate the steps you are taking ultimately determines your success.

Here's how:

First of all, I want you to notice that the evaluation is part of the process. I want you to always be asking yourself, *Am I headed in the right direction? Am I moving toward my 3× Vision, or am I staying the same? Are the steps that I'm taking on a regular basis moving me closer to my goal or farther away from my goal?*

I'm going to show you how to determine if you are headed in the right direction by teaching you my three-step evaluation process that you can start using right away. You're also going to learn how to determine if what you're focusing on right now doesn't actually matter. You're going to learn what to focus on instead.

MY THREE-STEP EVALUATION PROCESS

This is the evaluation process I use every week to stay on track for my goals. I learned it from my business coach, Stacey Boehman. It's quite simple but incredibly effective.

I need to check in again with you first. For this evaluation process to work, you have to actually use it. So I want to ask you, "Are you taking your professional development seriously?"

Now, if you're reading this book, my hope is that you are taking your professional development seriously. The truth is, many corporate leaders only think about career advancement once or twice per year. Then the rest of the time, you're focusing on doing a good job. That is why it's so important to make this evaluation process a regular part of your workweek.

The process starts with asking yourself, *Am I moving toward my 3× Vision for my career?* Asking yourself this question on a regular basis is going to transform your ability to actually make it into that next level of leadership.

Now I want to walk you through the three-step evaluation process. Grab a pen and paper and your 3× Vision. Reference your 3× Vision while looking back at your month.

Then write down:

1. What worked.
2. What didn't work.
3. What you can do differently.

It's important to put this on paper instead of just in your head so you can go back to what to do differently.

If you took a specific action this month toward your 3× Vision, you could also ask yourself, *Was that successful? Why was it successful? Why wasn't it successful? What was off about the conversation, and what would I do differently next time?*

Think about it. How many times have you felt really frustrated in your career and you didn't know what to do? Well, you're going to have that three-step evaluation to look at and say, "Oh, here's something that I can do tomorrow. I have that written down for myself."

Next, you're just going to decide what the next best action is. You're going to look at what you want to do differently, and you'll take action on one of those things.

STOP FOCUSING ON THE *FALSE* RED FLAGS

What you think is important in terms of advancing your career often doesn't actually matter. So you need to learn how to identify what isn't working so you can stop spinning your wheels in the wrong direction.

For example, up until now, you may have been thinking that a promotion is a reward for your hard work. So if you want to work even harder so you get a promotion (instead of focusing on your professional development), you will burn yourself out and still not get what you want.

Here's how to determine if you're focused on the wrong thing:

As you're working through the things that are going wrong, you might write something like: "I got assigned to the wrong project." Maybe you got assigned to a project that's not as strategic as you would have liked. Or you have a team and you don't really like them. Or you have a new boss and you don't really like them. Whatever that is, it's that something happened, and you're frustrated about it.

What I'm going to show you with each one of these is that the reason why they don't actually matter is because they're 100 percent in your control.

FALSE RED FLAG #1: YOU'RE GETTING ASSIGNED THE WRONG TYPE OF PROJECTS

This isn't a sign that you can't get promoted. It's just a sign that you're doing something wrong that you need to fix. You need to speak up. You need to have more strategic conversations, either with your boss or your boss's boss. You need to challenge yourself by asking, "What can I do differently in order to communicate the types of projects that I actually do want?"

That's why I say these aren't really red flags. They're just red flags to you to say that you need to do something different. But it doesn't mean that you're at the wrong organization or that things aren't going to work out for you here. Because that's an easy fix. You fix that, and you're going to get the right projects.

FALSE RED FLAG #2: GETTING PASSED OVER FOR A PROMOTION

I have a lot of clients who get passed over for a promotion. Something that they felt like they were a shoo-in for, and then somebody else gets the role. Either they hire outside of the organization, or they bring in someone from a different department. Whatever that is, it can feel really frustrating, and it could totally feel like a red flag. You can say, "Oh, well. This company just doesn't support me."

No! It actually means that you didn't advocate for yourself. You didn't show them you were ready for an executive position, and you didn't make it a no-brainer for them to put you into that role. That is all that it means. Fix that, and then you will be a shoo-in the next time a promotion opportunity opens up.

FALSE RED FLAG #3: YOU DON'T HAVE A SEAT AT THE TABLE

I know this can feel very frustrating. For example, I have clients who blamed the pandemic for them not having a seat at the table, because they were now working virtually. But you know what? You actually didn't have a seat at the table back then, because if you did, you'd *still* have a seat at the table.

It's a false idea to think that you just deserve a seat at the table. You have to go out and get it. It's not a red flag. It doesn't mean anybody is out to get you. It just means that you need to move forward and start building trust so that they bring you into those meetings. That's it.

FALSE RED FLAG #4: YOU HAVE DIFFICULTY SPEAKING UP

You can say that it's a red flag because they don't like you, or they don't listen to you, or nobody asks you any questions.

No! It simply means that you haven't learned the communication skills to interject yourself and start speaking up. That's all it means. It's not a red flag. It doesn't mean that you shouldn't work at this organization because everybody in the room is a man and you're a woman. It doesn't mean anything except that you need to learn how to speak up. You need to learn how to talk sooner. And you need to learn how to interject yourself into the conversation.

Now, I want to tell you that if you fix all four of these things, or even one of these things, then you will be building trust with the executive team that you can lead at that higher executive level.

If you're assigned to the right projects, you are building trust.

If you're getting rewarded for your hard work and you're getting looked at for promotion opportunities, you are building trust.

If you have a seat at the table, you are building trust.

If you're able to speak up and interject in meetings, you are building trust.

I want you to look at these things and look at them the right way. It's not that they're not important, but what we often do is we give up on our organization, or our team, or our boss, way too soon. These are completely within your control to fix.

THE REAL RED FLAGS YOU NEED TO LOOK OUT FOR

These are actual red flags. What I mean by a red flag is a hard stop. It's going to be really difficult to get through.

Now, the funny thing is you are probably looking at these things as not being a big deal. And they're the biggest deal. I really want this chapter to sink in.

The only two red flags are:

#1: **You're not receiving any feedback.**

#2: **You keep receiving the same feedback.**

These are really just variations on the same thing.

If you are soliciting feedback from your boss and they're not really able to articulate what you need to do to get yourself to the next level, that's a red flag.

If you're receiving the same feedback over and over again, it means that your boss has basically given up on you.

When your boss gives you this kind of feedback, it's usually something very generic that they can't really quantify. For example: You need to be more strategic. You need to speak up more. You need to get out of the weeds.

Then you start getting yourself out of the weeds. You start communicating differently. You start doing all of the things that we're talking about in these lessons, and they're still saying, "Well, you just need to do this."

Most of the time, it's not personal. Whenever you're getting no feedback or the same feedback over and over again, it basically means that they're not paying attention to you. They don't have your career path as a top priority for them. Because if they did, then they would be giving you constructive feedback, right? They would actually be working with you on a promotion plan for yourself.

HOW TO OVERCOME THESE RED FLAGS

So the question becomes, what do you do about it?

If your boss isn't giving you any feedback, the solution is simple. Stop trying to solve the problem with that person.

Let's just assume that your boss doesn't care about you, and you start to take matters into your own hands. That's when we get other allies on our side. We do this by speaking up in the leadership team meetings and by creating relationships with other people who actually do matter.

The same thing is true if your boss is giving you the same feedback. We keep trying to fight the same battle over and over and over again when there could be a side step available to solve the problem. That way, it wouldn't even matter if our boss kept giving us that same feedback.

This is so important. These are the two places where you're going to spend most of your time, and it's actually quite useless. So make sure you're receiving no feedback or that same feedback, then you need to figure out something that you can do differently.

HOW TO SHIFT PERCEPTION

When it comes to building relationships with the right people at work, one thing you need to understand is that perception equals reality. If the leadership team doesn't see you as someone who can make it to the executive level, that's reality. It's your responsibility to shift their perception and create a new reality.

There are two ways to shift perception.

#1: **Shifting the way that you see yourself.**

#2: Shifting the way others see you.

One of the reasons why people struggle to get promoted into senior executive leadership positions is because they're really good at their job. This sounds a little bit opposite, but hear me out. What's happening is that you're known as the subject matter expert. You're known as someone who is really great at your job. What do subject matter experts do? They rely on the details. They rely on being good at their job. And they work really, really hard.

I had two different clients who received the same feedback from their bosses. The feedback was that they were too slow. But here's the thing. They were not actually too slow in the delivery. They always deliver by their deadline. What this feedback points to is that they're too slow in their process.

Here's the advice that I gave both of them:

> The goal here is not to change your process. Your process works for you. You're very detail-oriented. You want to make sure that you get everything right, and that allows you to deliver on time. There is nothing wrong with this process. The feedback that you're receiving is simply the perception from other people and from your boss. Her perception is that you take "too long." Now, she would never say "drop the ball" or "don't have attention to detail." Of course not. What she's saying is you are too slow.

So I coached my clients to shift the perception that they were too slow. Here are the instructions I gave:

> You are going to give regular updates to your boss about your progress. You are going to tell your boss exactly where you are and give them updates. Now, these aren't going to go into the weeds. This is going to be more of a high level: "These are the three things I'm working on this week." You're not going to go into all the details about exactly what you're working on. What you're going to do is you're going to give more frequent updates.

When I mentioned this to both of these clients, they said, "Oh yeah. I never send my boss updates."

The problem is not that they're too slow. It's that they're leaving their bosses guessing. By the time it gets done, their bosses have spent so much time wondering if somebody is working on it or not. It's going to feel late because it is your boss's job on the line.

You have to realize that it's your boss's job to make sure you get this done. They don't want to micromanage you. They don't want to watch you every step of the way. What they do want is to make sure it gets done. When they feel like it's going too slow, they worry that you're not going to meet your deadline.

You see where I'm going here. Both of them agreed to give more frequent updates to their boss about their status along the way. I called this concept "Showing Your Work."

You've heard about this in grade school that we all need to show our work. That's what our teacher requires. Then somehow, once we get into the corporate world and once we get into our working life, we forget to show our work.

There's a lot of legitimate reasons for this. First of all, we don't think it's necessary because it seems obvious. You might think, *Of course. Trust me. I always meet my deadlines.* So we don't think it's necessary to give these updates along the way.

The second thing is that we don't want to show that we're struggling. Because in the process of this being too slow, we're trying to figure something out. We don't have the answers yet, and that's okay. You don't have to have the answers yet. You just have to communicate something like: "I'm working on it," or "This is what I'm thinking," or "I should have it for you by Tuesday." You just want to *over*communicate a little while to build trust, and then we'll figure out how to trim back later.

The first step is to overcommunicate. Once you do that, you're going to notice that your boss no longer sees you as someone who's too slow. You're going to start to get feedback like, "Wow, you're really on top of things." That's the feedback you want to be receiving.

This is what I'm talking about here in this perception equals reality. It is the perception that other people have of you and that, in truth, is actually reality. And we want to fix the problem.

"YOU CAN'T GET PROMOTED BECAUSE OF X…"

This one happens a lot. For example, your boss gives you feedback that you can't get promoted because they haven't seen you lead a large team. But, you know you could lead a large team. However, their perception is that they've never seen you lead a large team.

This can feel super frustrating and very defeating. It can make you feel really small. Your solution might be the answers to these questions: "How do I lead a large team? How do I actually fix the problem that they're speaking about?"

But this isn't the right approach. The actual solution is: "How do I shift their perception of me so they trust I *can* lead a large team?" This feels a lot less frustrating, right?

Here's how to do it.

The first step in this example is to check in with your emotions. Ask yourself, *How am I feeling? Do I feel super frustrated? Do I feel defeated? Do I feel like this is a catch-22? Do I feel like I can't do anything about it?* If that's how you feel, stop. Realize that it doesn't have to be that way.

You don't have to change the literal thing that's happening. You don't have to lead a large team.

But what you do need to do is shift the perception. When you shift that perception for your boss, for the leadership team, for your CEO, for your team, for your peers…whenever you start to shift their perception, guess what? That actually becomes your reality.

All it takes is a simple shift. It simply says, "Oh, I see. The perception is that I'm not capable of leading a large team. I have to show them that I'm capable."

The next thing I want you to do is understand that this is true. This is their belief. There is nothing wrong with their perception of you. When we're thinking about being frustrated and trying to take action from that place of frustration and feeling defeated, it's going to be nearly impossible to break out of it. You just want to accept it as truth. There is a perception, and it's fine that they think that. I can't lead a large team. It's simply their perception. It doesn't actually mean I cannot lead a large team.

Do you see what I'm saying here? It doesn't mean that you're not capable of being a senior vice president or a CFO. Just because they don't see you that way does not mean that you're not capable of it. But you need to take their perception as truth, and then you have to show them.

The next thing I want you to do is just make adjustments along the way. You're going to shift your behaviors. You're going to say, "Okay, did that shift the perception at all?" Next, you're going to start asking. You're going to get feedback from your boss. You're going to find ways to figure out if your perception is shifting.

Now, here's the kicker. And this is so, so hard. Not everybody is going to see all of the actions that you're taking. You're shifting this perception with your boss. But let's say the other half of the leadership team has not seen it. They still have that old perception of you that you're the subject matter expert and you're not capable of higher executive leadership roles.

It gets really hard when, two years into this work, someone comes up to you and says, "Oh, I'm surprised. You now have a big team." Sure, they don't mean any harm. They're just literally surprised because they didn't see you as a leader. They always saw you as a subject matter expert.

Just be very careful that as you're doing this work, and as you're shifting this behavior and shifting people's perception, know that there's always going to be somebody who didn't get on the train. That didn't follow the boat. And you're just going to have to evaluate your progress along the way.

So keep asking yourself, *Does it feel like I'm moving closer toward my goal of being in a senior executive leadership role?*

If not, get feedback from people. It could be from a coach, a mentor, a sponsor, your peers. Just make sure you're communicating with other people and getting feedback along the way so you can understand and adjust your path.

Once you implement some of the strategies I've laid out in this book, you will begin to shift the perception at your organization about anything. Whether the perception is that you're somebody who's difficult to work with, you're somebody who is not capable of an executive leadership role, you're somebody who is too slow, or you're somebody who doesn't speak up enough. Whatever it is that you're trying to work on, you'll be able to shift that perception so that the executive team will say, "You know what? She is ready. Let's promote her now. We need her in a higher executive-level role."

CHAPTER SUMMARY

- Understanding how to properly evaluate the steps you are taking ultimately determines your success.

- The three-step self-evaluation process is: look back at your month and write down: 1) What worked; 2) What didn't work; and 3) What you can do differently.
- What we think is important in terms of advancing our careers often doesn't actually matter, so stop focusing on false flags. False flags include: 1) You're getting assigned the wrong type of projects; 2) Getting passed over for a promotion; 3) You don't have a seat at the table; and 4) You have difficulty speaking up.
- There are only two REAL red flags that you need to look out for. They are: 1) You're not receiving any feedback; and 2) You keep receiving the same feedback.
- You can overcome these REAL red flags by *shifting perception*. There are two ways to shift perception: 1) Shifting the way that you see yourself; and 2) Shifting the way others see you.

ACTION STEPS

I want you to keep these strategies at the forefront of your mind. If at any point you are struggling and you're wondering what to do next, the answer lies in one of these three things:

1. Are you having better conversations with your boss by speaking to the vision? Remember that getting out of the weeds is as much about the way that you communicate as it is time management.

- Ask yourself, *How am I communicating to leadership? How am I communicating to teams? Am I thinking about the strategy, the vision, the three pillars, and what we need to accomplish today?*

2. Are you building confidence in your ability to lead at a higher executive level by making decisions from your 3× Vision? Remember that to get promoted into senior executive leadership, you need to think like a senior executive leader now.

   - Ask yourself, *What is that big vision? Where am I headed?* Don't just focus on the next promotion. If you find yourself getting hung up on what the next thing is and what it's going to take to get there, you're going to feel frustrated and stuck. So go bigger. That's going to show you what you need to start doing today to make it to even that next level of leadership.

3. Are you building trust with the executive team? Remember that your boss can't be the only person who supports your promotion. The senior executive team must also believe that you are ready to lead at a higher executive level.

   - Ask yourself, *Am I building trust with the right people? Am I having 15-Minute Ally Meetings? How am I communicating with them?*

4. More powerful reflection questions to ask yourself:

   - *Do you have the courage to put yourself forward and to actually advance your career? Are you advocating for yourself or waiting to be asked?*

- *Do you understand your own unique leadership style, and have you communicated that with others?*
- *Do you have a strategy for a promotion?*
- *Are you reviewing your Promotion Blueprint every month? Do you know what to do next? Are you spending time every single month on that strategy?*

If you keep doing these steps, over and over and over again, you *will* see results, and you *will* get promoted.

Download free resource guides at stacymayer.com/resources.

CHAPTER 11

OVERCOMING YOUR FEAR OF FAILURE

Now that you have the strategies you need to advance to the senior executive level, you need to understand another thing that stands in your way:

Your fear of *failure.*

Failure is part of your daily life as an executive leader. You're putting yourself out there. So it's important that you get comfortable with failure now.

As you are taking the steps outlined in this book, I also want you to start asking yourself, *Am I willing to take risks? How can I mitigate those risks? What are the ways that I can solve for the potential risks?*

Understand worst-case scenarios. Ask yourself, *How might I fail? What is the worst thing that could happen here?* Then plan accordingly. Actually plan for those obstacles and those risks.

Then ask yourself, *If I fail, then what? If I fail at this project, what will happen? What are the different levels of failure? Is it likely that I will fail?* Getting curious about failure and owning the fact that it's a possibility is going to help you be a lot more comfortable going for things.

According to The Life Coach School founder Brooke Castillo, life is fifty–fifty. We experience 50 percent positive emotions and 50 percent negative emotions.

If life is fifty–fifty, no matter what we do, we're not striving to go and advance in our career because life is going to be great and it's going to be easy. We're actually striving to advance in our career strictly for growth. Strictly to become a better human being, to challenge ourselves, and to have a bigger impact, because those rewards are also the same as the failures. We're starting to learn how to get more and more comfortable with it and really make a choice—I'm going to go for this. I'm going to do something different.

PASSIVELY FAILING VS. ACTIVELY FAILING

Part of this choice is the difference between passively failing and actively failing. I am one of those people who has always been pretty comfortable with failure. I identify as somebody who was very willing to take risks.

I moved to New York City without knowing a single person in the city. I had never even visited before. I got off the plane, and that was my first introduction to New York. I had no apartment, but I did have a couch to stay on that first night. That was pretty much it.

I knew I was taking a risk. I knew that it was risky to move to New York City. I also knew that I could handle it, I would figure it out, and I would be resourceful.

But what if I moved to New York City and I passively failed, as in: "I'm going to go to New York City, but it's probably not going to work out. I don't want to get my hopes up. We'll just see what happens." What if I used that language with myself and I did fail in New York?

If I passively failed, I wouldn't have been able to learn from my failure. Because that's the problem with passively failing. We blame our actions on other people, situations, circumstances, and things that are not within our control.

But active failure is taking full ownership of your failure. This is a really good thing, because when you take ownership, you also must acknowledge that this means you have the power to do something about it.

So, let's take a look at these two different types of failure. Are you passively failing or actively failing?

For example, let's say you have that mindset: "We'll just see what happens." Maybe you're going to have a conversation with your boss or speak up at the leadership team meeting. But instead you think, *I'll just see what happens.* Notice the only difference between these two phrases is "I" versus "we." When you think, *We'll just see what happens*, it's as if it doesn't even matter what *you* do.

But instead, an active failure would be: "I'm going to go for it. I'm going to speak up at this meeting. I'm going to have a skip-level conversation. I am going to see what happens. AND I'm going to identify what happened by asking myself, *How did that go?*"

Passively failing is saying things to yourself like: *It doesn't really matter.* So we say that to make ourselves feel better.

Instead, say to yourself, "If this doesn't work out, I will find something else." I said that a lot when I moved to New York. I really went for it. But if it didn't work out, I would move somewhere else. I could go back to where I was before. It doesn't matter. That is true. But the attitude that comes behind "It really doesn't matter what I do. It doesn't matter what happens" means that you're passively failing. You're not going to be able to learn from your mistakes.

I don't know what to do.

We say this a lot to ourselves. Like, if I only knew what to do, then I could do something different. But in truth, you always know something, right? You always know one thing. So if you're not sure which project to take, or what to do to get a promotion, or who to talk to, or what to say to your boss, ask yourself, *What DO I know?*

"I don't want to get my hopes up."

So you don't really go for whatever opportunity it is because you're afraid that you're going to get too upset if it doesn't work out. We don't want to get our hopes up like on Christmas morning, that sort of excited energy. We don't want to get too excited about it in case it doesn't work out. So instead, tell yourself, *If they say no, I will be okay.*

If you have an emotional reaction when things don't work out, you get really devastated, so then work on that. Say, "'Okay, this time, instead of not going for it or not getting my hopes up, I'm going to do something different so that I can manage my emotions after it doesn't work out right." It's a little bit of a different way of thinking about it, but it makes a huge difference.

Active failure is owning your part, your responsibility, and evaluating your failures afterward. That is how we learn from our mistakes. Active failure always gets you closer to your goals, and passive failure may or may not.

CHANGE MANAGEMENT AS PART OF YOUR JOB DESCRIPTION

Another way that you're going to get more and more comfortable with taking bold risks and taking big action is really understanding that change management is part of your job description. As you move into higher levels of executive leadership, doing hard things is part of your job description. You need to anticipate change and anticipate obstacles. It's part of what you do.

By becoming the Executive Ahead of Time, you are essentially taking leadership responsibility. You understand that you need to do something different, you need to put yourself out there, you need to deliberately manage your career and have growth as a core value if you want to advance.

As you can start to take ownership of your career, when you have situations happen at work that feel challenging or different, you'll easily be able to handle them. They will feel like it's part of your job.

WHAT FEAR OF FAILURE ACTUALLY IS

Ultimately, deep down, what is happening when we're afraid of something? We feel like we're afraid to put ourselves out there. We're afraid to have those difficult conversations. We have a fear of being kicked out of the group, of being ostracized, of not having friends at work.

Let's say you put yourself out there, and the CEO calls you in to have a conversation with them. As a result, you get really excited, and you and the CEO are bouncing really great ideas off of each other. The experience feels really supportive and strong.

Later in an all-hands meeting, the CEO mentions you and this conversation that they had with you and how excited they were about that conversation and some of the ideas that you brought up. Now, some of your peers get very jealous. They feel uncomfortable around you. Maybe they even tease you or say rude things to you, such as, "Well, who do you think you are for going and having a conversation with the CEO?"

You feel like you just got kicked out of the "club." That's what you're so afraid of. This actually happened to one of my Executive Ahead of Time students, and she came to our group coaching call wishing that she had never set up the meeting with her CEO in the first place.

Who is in charge of your career, ultimately? Is it your peers? Honestly, ask yourself about that. Yes, we do want to get along with people. We need to be able to get along with people at our jobs. But just being afraid that they might be jealous of you is not enough reason to not have the conversation with your CEO.

There is always another group of people, another culture, another organization, and another opportunity waiting for you.

THE CASE FOR MANAGING YOUR EMOTIONS

As you begin to take on higher levels of responsibility at your company, the stakes are also going to feel higher.

I once received an email from a corporate leader who had been advocating for resources, but kept getting turned down. She felt that every time she made some progress forward, something in her organization pushed her back.

She had received a promise that she would be able to build out a team, and then management came down from the top and took that away from her.

So when she emailed me, she felt like she had just been given a demotion, and she was very frustrated. She also had a brand-new boss she has to work with, and it just felt very hopeless for her.

But here's the kicker. She worked hard to get where she is. She is proud of her job. She wants to stay at her company.

Here is what I told her: "Stop fighting so hard."

This is what I mean. We have to, as senior executive leaders, learn how to get the big picture and think strategically.

SUGGESTION #1

My first suggestion for her in terms of managing her emotions was to stop. She's trying to solve this problem with frustration and annoyance. She's basically giving up on her growth mindset. So I advised her to slow down.

Let's stop asking for the team because the way you're asking isn't working. Let's really look at what's happening in the organization. Stop talking and slow down. I advised her to continue doing her job and to take all that frustration and put it in a metaphorical box.

Instead of feeling frustrated, she's going to focus on other things. What is the impact that she has actually made? Why does she like working at this organization?

This isn't just positive thinking. This is actually telling her why she is doing what she's doing. It's reminding her of what actually matters.

So she should really think about: What are those wins? What

are the things that she has actually accomplished? What are the ways that she can do more of that?

SUGGESTION #2

The other thing that I want her to look at is: What can she stop doing? She's spinning her wheels trying to prove to the leadership team that she's really, really great. She's thinking, *If I can do more work, then I can show them that I need more support.*

But I want her to think more strategically and see the big picture. I want her to stop doing a few things and stop going to that meeting. Slow down. Figure out what actually matters.

SUGGESTION #3

The third thing I wanted her to do was to figure out on her own, with her current resources, with her current situation, how she can begin delegating.

Delegating doesn't have to mean to a person. If she feels like she has nobody to delegate to, she can delegate to something else. She can delegate to the ether. She can delegate to the next year. Whatever that is for her, she needs to get smart.

WHAT WILL HAPPEN WHEN YOU BETTER MANAGE YOUR EMOTIONS

Here's the thing. If she starts managing her emotions, if she stops feeling frustrated, if she starts looking at what's actually working and really understands how to prioritize and how to think more strategically, she will become the Executive Ahead of Time. She'll feel better. She'll start to make a bigger impact. She'll have actual influence at her organization.

Now, she can really look at the situation and say, "Maybe I do actually want to leave this organization now." But she's going to make that choice from an empowered place. She's going to know, and she'll say, "Okay, I've tried. I worked on this. I have become that Executive Ahead of Time. And my next steps are simply a choice."

So now I want you to take action. The next time you try something new outside of your comfort zone, something that feels a little bit risky, I want you to really check in with your thoughts about it.

Am I really going for it? And am I going all in?

By all in, you could also choose not to go for it. That is a choice. Am I really choosing something, or am I passively failing and not going for that risk?

CHAPTER SUMMARY

- Getting comfortable with failure is the final step to claiming your seat at the table.

- To get comfortable with failure, I want you to start asking yourself, *Am I willing to take risks? How can I mitigate those risks? What are the ways that I can solve for these risks? If I fail, then what happens? What are the different levels of failure?*

- The difference between passively failing and actively failing is when we *passively* fail, we blame our failure on things we cannot control (other people, situations, and circumstances). When we *actively* fail, we take full ownership of our failure. Doing so requires us to acknowledge that we have the power to do something about it.

- Another way that you're going to get more and more comfortable with taking bold risks and taking big actions is understanding that change management is part of your job description as a senior executive leader.

- Becoming the Executive Ahead of Time means learning from your failures and advocating for yourself. It means understanding your unique leadership values so you can put yourself out there as your true, authentic, powerful self.

CONCLUSION

"If you look really closely, most overnight successes take a long time."

—STEVE JOBS

Congratulations, corporate badass! After implementing what you have learned in this book, you will officially be able to say that you are on your way to becoming a senior executive leader.

But becoming a senior executive leader is not an overnight journey. This is something that you're going to be building on for some time now.

You might receive a promotion very quickly. You might be able to make it into your 3x Vision in half the time. But that doesn't mean this isn't a journey. You still have twenty years left of your career. So that is why you're going to be building out over the next twenty years—so you can, with time, step into your true, authentic power.

Your organization needs you in a senior executive leadership role. It's important for you to learn these skills and to learn how to become the Executive Ahead of Time. Once you make it into that senior executive leadership role, that's when your voice is going to be heard. That's when you're going to be able to make the impact that you really want to be making at your organization. That's when your work is really going to matter at your organization. You're really going to be able to see the fruits of your labor, and it's going to feel really good to go to work.

I received a note a few weeks ago from a client who suggested that she was tired of "chasing the title," and I get it. So many corporate women feel like they don't want to put on a persona. They don't want to be inauthentic. And I want to show you right here, right now, that your authentic self *is* powerful. You are a very powerful, very capable human being. You are willing and able to do hard things.

Don't diminish your power in an effort to be more likable. That's just confusing. It's confusing everybody. It's confusing you. You feel bad about yourself, and it confuses leadership because they don't know how to recognize you for your true value that you have to offer the organization.

Always keep in mind, "If you want to be more authentic, be more powerful." In essence, your authentic self is extremely powerful. You have the power to make the changes you want to see at your organization today. Whether that's incorporating more diverse perspectives or simply making sure every voice in the room is valued and heard.

I want you to understand this. Corporate women often don't want to own their power because so often, to them, power has looked like having power *over* other people—being in charge of others, telling people what to do, being a boss instead of a leader. And you don't aspire to be that kind of leader.

You want to have power *with* other people. You don't want to live in a world where you have power *over* them, and neither do I.

I trust that if you are reading this book that your heart is in the right place. You want to have power *with* other people. You are an *inclusive* leader. You care about your organization. You want your work to actually matter. Know that it's okay to step up and own your authentic power. You are not like your predecessors.

Even if it feels unfamiliar, that is why we do this work for ourselves. We mitigate our risks. We understand how to learn from our failures. We learn how to advocate for ourselves. We understand our unique leadership values so that we can put ourselves out there in a way that is really authentic and very true. We're not pretending to be somebody else. We're just showing our true, authentic, powerful selves.

I want to encourage you, as you continue to think about this work and continue to think about moving into higher-level executive positions, that you have the courage to face your fears. Remind yourself that you are fully capable of doing hard things and that your legacy matters. Once you get yourself into a higher-level executive position, that's when you'll be able to make the change that you really want to be making in this world.

You are a brilliant manager. Your team loves you. You know you are capable of doing more. Once you implement the steps in the book, it will no longer be a matter of IF you will be promoted but WHEN you will be promoted.

I can't wait to see what you can accomplish once you get there.